Outgrowing the Shackles

A journal of two journeys.

Helen Pollard

Onwards and Upwards Publishers

3 Radfords Turf, Cranbrook, Exeter,
EX5 7DX, United Kingdom.
www.onwardsandupwards.org

This first edition published in the United Kingdom by Onwards and Upwards Publishers (2018).

ISBN:	978-1-78815-669-1
Typeface:	Sabon LT
Photography:	Charis Baker (p.3) / Helen Pollard (p.23)
Graphic design:	LM Graphic Design

Printed in the United Kingdom.

About the Author

 Helen, sixty-five, survived a traumatic childhood through Jesus' miraculous healing and help from secular therapies and varied prayer ministries. The only one of nine to complete an arduous five-and-a-half-year course leading to an honours degree in Sociology / Social Admin and qualifications as a State Registered Nurse and a Certificated Health Visitor, she was keenly interested in mental health. As a health visitor she helped people in emotional need; as a nurse of children, and babies in intensive care, she particularly supported her patients' families.

Helen married Steve in 1979. Sadly, their first son, Joe, died after thirty minutes. Their other three are thriving Christians, married, and have produced six delightful grandchildren. After struggling with several cancers and other illnesses, Helen responded to God's call to become a counsellor. She is trained in psychotherapy, holds a Diploma in Life Business and Executive Coaching and a further degree in Eclectic Counselling. She has practised for over thirty years in both secular counselling and coaching, and in prayer ministry.

In 2010 God led Helen and Steve to combine their prayer ministry experience and therapeutic training in the ministry *Bespoke Growth in God* which now serves churches, marriages and individuals nationwide. Written following requests from many clients, and another call from God, this book combines the story of Helen's childhood and early adulthood with insights and tools honed in that ministry. Helen's desire is to enable those in seemingly impossible circumstances to press into, and find hope in, God.

You can find out more about *Bespoke Growth in God* from the website: *www.bespokepollards.com*

Or scan the QR-barcode with your mobile phone.

3

Endorsements

A beautifully written book that both breaks your heart and fills it with hope all at the same time. A story of deep pain and brokenness, but also of a God whose redemptive love and healing power is always reaching out to restore all things.

Nicola Neal
CEO and Founder, Every Life International

Helen has a tremendous empathy for others. I met her when struggling in my own life. Her care, questions and guidance helped me find hope and encouragement that God can work in and through the most trying of circumstances. Now I've read her story, I can see that she embodies this because she herself has lived it.

Andy Croft
Soul Survivor

What a truly brilliant and beautiful book. It is both heart-rending and heart-filling. Somehow Helen has managed to write in a way that is very real about the pain and struggles whilst making it so uplifting, encouraging and inspiring. She leaves me wanting to praise God in every chapter.

I love the twin threads of her autobiography interspersed with snapshots of life today. In talking so honestly of her ongoing struggles, she manages to weave in incredible nuggets of wisdom and teaching in such an engaging and helpful way.

Just reading this book is to encounter her profound ministry wisdom and insights as well as to meet God's truth in fresh ways. This book will bring immense hope and understanding to many. It gripped me from the beginning and leaves me gripped by the wonder of God's love and healing.

Rev. James Grier
Leader of Unlimited Church
Diocesan Youth Church Adviser

This book is a riveting read – one that I believe will be an immense blessing, as well as an eye-opener, to many.

As Helen tells her story, she regularly pauses to express the difficulties that she feels in describing the events that unfold. It's sometimes hard for those who have not had the experience of abuse to realise that it is not something you can altogether leave behind – even after years of healing. In this way, Helen effectively conveys the ongoing pain of her abuse, whilst at the same time testifying to the reality of the healing that is possible.

This book has raised a host of questions for me and given fascinating insights into Helen's experience. I am sure it will help a great many people.

Canon Rev. David McInnes

This is a truly remarkable book. Helen has written with great insight and honesty the story of her extremely abusive childhood. Helen has been truthful about her feelings and her breakdowns whilst wisely avoiding any lurid details of sexual abuse. This has been cleverly combined with her present-day story of writing the book. Ultimately, however, this is the story of how Jesus' miraculous healing love leads to freedom.

A book of hope for any reader needing healing and transformation from previous abuse.

Dr Lin Button
Founder of The Healing Prayer School

This book gripped me from the start. It is a story of courage, hope and healing in the most difficult circumstances of life. Helen is deeply honest about her feelings then and now. She is a person of immense faith, wisdom and insight. Reading this makes me thankful for the amazing grace of Jesus. This is not an easy read, but it is powerful and a real testimony to the power of God's love overcoming evil and strongholds. Helen is a trophy of grace. Thank you for writing and sharing so powerfully.

Malcolm Macdonald
Vicar, St Mary's Loughton

Contents

AUTHOR'S NOTE 8

PREFACE 9

FOREWORD 15

PART ONE.. 17

1. Spare child 19

2. Training begins 26

3. Move to Lorrisford 29

4. Life in the village improves.................................... 32

5. Gran dies 37

6. The horrendous week.. 41

7. New friends 44

8. Rage released 48

9. Darkness increases 52

10. Pinpricks of light... 55

11. God is real 58

12. A painful interlude 62

13. Jonty enjoyed.. 67

14. Jonty spoilt 70

15. Jonty lost 79

16. Aftermath 81

17. No more visits to the village 85

18. Downs and ups 89

19. Grandpa dies.. 93

20. Cast out but taken up... 96

PART TWO.. **99**

21. First breakdown...101

22. Second breakdown...105

23. Recovery begins..109

PART THREE **115**

24. Further healing 117

25. The move to university in the south.....................120

26. The beginning of "rules to relationship" 128

27. Descent into depression.....................................131

28. Crisis and comfort 134

29. Learning He is always enough............................142

30. Final return to the south 146

31. 10th March 155

32. My operation...161

33. I recover 165

APPENDIX 169

Author's Note

The names of people and places in this book have been changed to protect their identity.

Preface

There is a condition known as hyperacusis, a debilitating hearing disorder characterized by an increased sensitivity to certain frequency and volume ranges of sound. To sufferers, everyday sounds easily tolerated by others are painfully loud. In contrast, I am discovering that my husband Steve, at sixty-six, is finding it harder to hear. We stopped watching a programme one night recently because he couldn't hear the dialogue which was plain to me.

What has this to do with *Outgrowing the Shackles?* Just as people differ in their tolerance to sound so that what is acceptable to one is debilitating to another, so each one of us has a different tolerance for many of the experiences that impinge upon us. An experience which could be a fettering shackle to one may not affect the freedom of another. Similarly, a person who has not suffered experiences that everyone would recognise as traumatic may nonetheless have suffered experiences which cause them to be living restricted by shackles similar to those another began to wear following trauma. I have heard people say, in effect, "I shouldn't have these problems because nothing really bad has happened to me." This book is written for everyone who finds they are not living the abundant life Jesus promised but in some way or other are fettered by shackles. It does not matter why or how you began to wear your particular shackles; the Jesus who enabled me to outgrow mine can bring release to anyone.

So, although my shackles originated from experiences of abuse that are thankfully outside the common experience, I am not writing yet another book about abuse. This is a book about hope.

I have repeatedly been told that I should write my story because many people would find it helpful – one client even offered to pay for the book's publication – but I have been reluctant to do so. This is partly because several people, some still alive, may well not recognise the part they played in my story. They may even be caused some distress. To them I can only say that I have written as truthfully and lovingly as possible, refraining from as much detail as I could whilst still being honest.

Another reason is that I recognise that my experiences are, fortunately, not part of an ordinary childhood and so may sound far-fetched to some. These experiences are, however, not as rare as many would wish to believe. Whilst practising as a therapist I have worked with one client who was abused in the same village I was, and another who suffered similar experiences in another city where I lived. For professional reasons, I did not self-disclose to them.

I have also been reluctant because I am aware that stories such as mine can be perversely attractive to those drawn to the "dark side". I do not in any way want to glorify or excite interest in the shameful things some people do, or to encourage an unseemly attraction for some to the horrors inflicted.

Yet I also know there are others who have suffered as I have, who may even now be mired in the dark loneliness and torment which continue long after the actual abuse may have stopped. For others still, this abuse may be a present reality. I have written my story for you who fall into these categories. I want you to see that there is a power far greater than any power that has abused you; a love that is deeper than any hatred you have suffered; a comfort that can assuage your pain; a very real hope of a fulfilled life in place of the despair and hopelessness that seem now to be your future.

I have found this power, love, comfort, and hope in Jesus. He has patiently rescued, healed, and restored me. At his cross I have found forgiveness for myself and for my abusers; healing for my physical, sexual, emotional, and spiritual wounds; a way into a fulfilled life as a wife, mother, grandmother, and counsellor/prayer minister. Most of all, I have found a constant friend in Jesus. If my story helps one person to find similar relief in Him then it has been worth all the very real struggle it has been to write.

My desire is that as you read you will gain insight into how we begin to wear shackles, often from childhood experiences, and the effect that they have; that you will see how therapy, prayer ministry, and the love and support of Jesus can enable you to outgrow these; most of all, my desire is that you will find hope.

Necessarily my story runs chronologically from birth onwards. I have not written it as a movement from one experience of God's grace and healing to another, a story of victory and release. Although that would be encouraging, it could also be misleading; it might encourage people to think that God removed my shackles one after another, and therefore wonder what is wrong with them, that they have an ongoing struggle for which the longed-for freedom seems to be so elusive. My journey has not been a series of God encounters, be it at a festival, conference, or in private prayer, where God has removed my shackles one after another. Rather it has been a journey of darkness and light, advance and setback, with God at times very present and at others seeming distant, but throughout that journey enabled by him to outgrow my shackles.

As can be the case for all who have suffered, daily life can bring painful resonances. This was especially true for me as I began to write this book. Despite receiving years of therapy and also significant healing from Jesus, the events I recall are still so painful that I found it impossible to write this as a straightforward chronological account. I was only able to write for about thirty minutes each day by asking the Lord, "What do you want me to write today?" although occasionally I was able to write for longer. Often the pain of revisiting these memories meant that I needed several days' recuperation before I was able to continue. As I wrote about my journey into and out of my shackles from abuse, and into a transfigured life, I travelled another journey. For that reason, this book is subtitled *A Journal of Two Journeys;* it includes the chronological journey of abuse and recovery, and the journey of writing with all its struggles. In that journey, I have shared some of the understanding and tools that I – and many others – have found helpful. To make the distinction between the two journeys clear, I have adopted the simple formula of using normal type when referring to my past story and italics when referring to my writing journey.

Originally, I expected to write in stages, eventually producing three books covering my life to the present day, as I believed it would be too painful in one go. I thought I had finished this first book at the end of Part One but I was led to write Part Two about the two breakdowns I had in my twenties, and then to write linking chapters to connect these first two sections. The end product was somewhat chaotic. I was then helped to produce a sharper sense and rhythm in the chronological journey but for me that seemed to lose the expression of the closeness I had had with God in the writing journey and also the true sense of just how turbulent the journey into – and out of – depression and mental torment can be.

My personal experience, and that of clients to whom I have ministered, is that when shackled, from whatever cause, you can feel as if the floorboards of an upper room have been removed and you are struggling to stay aloft on the one or two that remain. Depression and breakdown can feel like even those boards have collapsed, and you are lying in a heap of ruins. When God begins to heal us, He knows just which particular memory to replace with comfort and truth so we can begin to have a safe place on which to stand. I have never yet seen Him do this chronologically. Instead, He begins to rebuild a sense of self in the ways that the person can handle. This can seem chaotic, and my attempt to create a more accessible structure made me realise that this is not a book I want to be read for its excitement. Rather, I want it to be an authentic sharing of both the journeys I've been on so that it might bring hope to other people. For those who have journeyed, or are journeying, through abuse or other restrictive experience towards recovery, it may help you to see from my writing journey that the road you travel may not be as straight and direct as some might imply, but, through the twists and turns, the ups and downs, Jesus will guide, strengthen, comfort, and help you as He heals. It is these two journeys which I place before you and invite you to travel with me.

When we are very young we are dependent upon others. Often it is in these early relationships that we become shackled. We lose, or may never grow into, a valid sense of self-worth and identity. We can live in dependence or codependence. In therapeutic terms, we suffer from attachment issues. Every child is born dependent but God's plan is that they grow into the 'Self' He designed them to be before the foundation of the world, learn a proper independence and then are able to become interdependent within family, work, church, and society. To the extent that a person remains bound by shackles they are inhibited from healthy interdependence and continue to suffer from attachment issues. As our society has increasingly moved into post-modern self-fulfilment with consequent breakdown of marriage, family and societal cohesion, I have become increasingly aware of the prevalence of attachment issues within our churches. As the National Health Service becomes stretched, there are more people coming into our churches who are seriously shackled. One of my hopes for this book is that those readers who may not identify with my story will be able to gain understanding and skills which will enable them to help others within our church and society.

I need to warn you that even with minimal detail there are points in my story that some may find distressing. Society is increasingly aware of these issues, and since the uncovering of abuse by Jimmy Savile more stringent safeguarding requirements have been put in place. I have complied with these and informed the relevant police authorities.

This book is made possible by the loving care I received from many people, especially my amazing husband Steve, my accepting and encouraging children, a whole team of patient, kind, and devoted ministers and mentors, my precious Grandpa, and my incomparable Jesus. To Him be all the glory, and to me be any mistakes.

Outgrowing the Shackles

Foreword by Rev. Canon John Hughes

Helen's story is an extraordinary journey from darkness to light. The darkness Helen was subjected to is beyond our comprehension and she opens a window into a world of ritual abuse and immense cruelty that no child should have to experience.

In the midst of her painful and courageous journey there are some wonderful gleams of light such as a loving Christian Grandpa who modelled fatherhood, a husband's faithful love, and a pastor who listened, prayed and brought the comfort of God.

Helen expresses with stark honesty the journey to discover God's healing, which has been a long process in which she has welcomed Christ's light and truth. It reveals the immense power of forgiveness and the hard choices she has made.

This story is a tribute to Helen's determination to find freedom and God's power to restore. It is a beautiful message of hope triumphing over darkness.

Outgrowing the Shackles

PART ONE

Part One

1

Spare child

My father's parents – Gran and Grandpa – were both Christians. Grandpa was the tenth child in a faithful Christian family and many of his relatives were missionaries.

Gran's family history was much more complicated. Her family, the Granvilles, believed that a son needed to be born to "carry on the family name". Gran was one of three sisters – a dishonour in the generational line. A number of Granvilles had, over the years, been involved in extramarital affairs. It seems ironic that the name Granville meant so much when it actually gained its prestige through the destruction of marriage and family. Nevertheless, it mattered to Gran's relatives, and she grew up with a significant tendency to feel fear and inadequacy, with an open doorway for the enemy in terms of wrecked marriages and family.

> There are two family lines in our history. Through one come curses and disaster, through the other blessing. This is worthy of note. It is valuable to recognise the former so that you can bring them to the cross and through forgiveness and release prevent their continuing down your line. This is Christ's antidote to the fear some have about the effect of family traits and behaviours. It is also good to celebrate the wonder of blessings passed down a family line. My husband and I were truly blessed and set on a healthy course when the importance of passing down good things to our children was emphasised as being of equal importance to digging out the problems we had inherited. Our desire as a couple has been to build a dam for our children and

19

our children's children: a dam to hold back unhelpful patterns and practices from our past and a new platform of abundant blessing for generations to come. Whenever we pray into a client's past history and see God redeem whole families from past disasters, we make a point of waiting on the Holy Spirit to see the blessing He will give in place of the "curse". He never fails to bring clear blessing, so beautiful and personal to each and every child who asks Him.

Things were tough for Gran. She was happy to have two living children, a boy and a girl. Her third pregnancy was not welcomed, and my father, who was that child, often recounted the doctor's words to Gran, "You may be glad of this one, one day." The words would prove to be true, but not in a way that Gran might have hoped.

Sadly, Dad's older sister died, aged three or five. Before the village had a mains water supply, several youngsters lost their lives to typhoid, and Dad's sister, Philomena, was one of them.

Fear entered into Gran and the whole village – fear and a sense of being helpless and out of control. In times of grief and need, the enemy "comes in like a flood". It doesn't seem fair, but it's how he works. In their weakness, members of the village employed a water diviner to find pure, untainted water. This seemed a reasonable act. Water divining is practised all over the northern countryside, and sources of pure and healing water are believed to exist in a variety of places.

The trouble with water divining is that it's a first step away from faith in God, and it comes with a price. Gradually, fear overtook the village, and the enemy's demands and manipulation grew out of control. Gran and her neighbours lost their faith in God and bowed increasingly to manipulation. Gran became a leader in superstition and eventually bondage to satanic rituals, especially when her eldest son Simeon was shot down in a leafleting raid over Berlin and became an early casualty of World War II.

My father became her only child. Gran became bitter that the doctor's words had now come true. Rejection in his early years left him vulnerable to pleasing his mother in any way he could.

From Dad's stories, it was clear he enjoyed life as a country boy, working with horses, bird-watching, and helping his dad plant a forest. He was full of mischief at school, but bright – the school star at all sport, spotted for county level cricket, and a keen organist in his local church. He never spoke about joining his mum in the rituals after they lost his sister, a grief then compounded by the loss of his elder brother, whom he greatly admired. Not only did he lose his brother but his parents then refused to let him follow Simeon into the RAF. Dad joined the Army instead, where he played rugby and athletics in inter-service competitions and was in relatively safe Africa for most of his service. He returned home with a fund of stories and became a teacher.

Mum was the eldest of several girls. Her father was from a high class background but he rebelled and ended up an alcoholic rag-and-bone man prone to outbursts of violence. Family life seemed unsustainable and one day Mum was taken to a park by her mother and handed over to a lady who took her to a children's home, where she was to live for the rest of her childhood. One of her sisters was in the home for a while but was allowed to leave because she didn't like it. The youngest sister was the "baby", so she stayed near her mum with a neighbour. Despite being punished for doing homework, Mum passed her exams and became a governess for a leading family before also training as a teacher.

So Mum and Dad were both teachers, and they met after the end of the war. It's a lovely story of two young people asked to teach at either end of the school hall who fell in love. They were married in 1948 and moved in with Dad's family.

Dad had lost a brother and sister. Gran had lost a son and a daughter. So had Grandpa – but instead of turning to God as Grandpa did, Dad and Gran turned to idols, real idols of water divining, as well as to demonic rituals, deep superstition, and other religious bodies that were against Jesus Christ and all He did for us on the cross.

My mum's background was one of abuse and extreme cruelty in children's homes from the age of three. She also lost a brother and a fiancé. She was disturbed and damaged, and easily swayed by Dad and Gran.

Gran and Mum found my arrival in this world very difficult. Gran wanted a grandson to carry on the family name. Mum only wanted one child – my older sister, Annabella – so she could spoil her and keep her free from the jealousy she herself had felt so deeply. So I brought double trouble when I arrived alive and female. I dashed Gran's hopes and threatened my older sister's security. My mum asked me to stay out of the way as much as I could so as not to upset Annabella. She later told me that she had farmed me out to other carers as a baby so that she wouldn't kill me.

Home was Granville House, built and designed by Grandpa on the top of a half-mile hill in the north of England. On wet days, the house looked sad and grey. I've never liked houses covered in grey pebbledash, probably because I miss Grandpa so much, and because of memories from that place. Granville House did have some beautiful features. After all, Grandpa built and designed it himself and he loved God and all things beautiful. The lounge was oak-panelled with a roaring log fire and pretty turret windows. The hall had an oak floor and staircase and a large conservatory overlooking two of his gardens. From every room upstairs we were blessed with breathtaking views of the countryside and Grandpa's gardens.

He was a wise old man, so he built a bungalow in the grounds to house a couple who would look after him and Gran in their old age. The couple lived rent free, and were able to help with the gardens and offer necessary care. It seems like commendable forethought, but after World War I, fighting in the trenches and a walk home from France with consumption, Grandpa was refused care by his in-laws. This left him sad and a little bitter for a while, and I think he was determined not to be caught in that position again. He forgave his family in his latter years, offering one of the rejecting relatives respite in his house when she was alone and needy. Such forgiveness was a great example to me.

I spent most of my early years out in those beautiful gardens, with their orchard, salad and vegetable patch, greenhouse and water garden, three lawns and flower areas, rockery, yard, and bog garden. What more could an adventurous child desire? Well, actually I did desire more, and I got it. You see, Grandpa didn't like what went on in his house at night and the consumption he had contracted in World War I left him with breathing difficulties, so he made his bedroom in a shed at the top of the vegetable garden. This meant we met daily as long as we lived at his home, and every holiday we spent there, and that leads to one of the very best parts of my story.

Grandpa loved Jesus all his life, and remained faithful through the hardest of times. He gave me an inheritance that will last. It started one Christmas when I was two or three years old. Have you ever studied a Christmas rose? They have no thorns, just broad white petals which nurse a delicate yellow centre, like Mary holding her precious child.

Grandpa grew Christmas roses. Every December they'd pop up as the thick snow melted. We would walk together to the rockery and he'd tell me the real meaning of Christmas. Whilst no donkey is mentioned in the Gospels, there was definitely a donkey in our story, because Grandpa and I both loved animals.

In February, pure white snowdrops covered the rockery gardens and hid under the hedges. These spoke of forgiveness. "F" for February and for forgiveness. In time, Grandpa told me, I would need to forgive my parents and the village for many things, and I would need forgiving

as well, but Jesus had already made the way for complete purity. I could be pure white like snowdrops because of His death on the cross. All I remember is the open head of the snowdrop... open to Him and singing His praises and the pure fresh whiteness open to me. Understanding the cross came much, much later.

Spring heralded lots of yellow flowers. Grandpa called them "golden trumpeters", because Jesus is King over all death and evil, and the spring bursts forth with new life after all hope seems to have gone in winter. In the same way, Jesus broke through at Easter when all hope seemed gone. Baby chickens and lambs, calves, and rabbits added to the story, along with beautiful blue tits and chaffinches eating from hanging coconuts. New life and fresh hope, never fading, was all I needed to know about Easter.

The summer flowers came in a myriad of colours. These spoke of God's love of beauty and His love for me and His care and guidance in every detail of my life. Even down to the clothes I chose. "If it fits in nature, it'll fit on you because God's design is perfect," was Grandpa's simple style-coaching advice and I've never proved him wrong. It saddens me sometimes to see how we even modify the colours of flowers these days. Look at natural colours – Grandpa's right – they always go well together.

These days with Grandpa would have been wonderful if the nights hadn't, in bitter contrast, been times of horror as Gran and Dad increasingly involved me in their satanic rituals. On numerous occasions

I was left sore and bleeding and exhausted after experiences many a child wouldn't have survived. I was blessed with a strong body and a strong will. I did survive and eventually I was rescued.

What is there to survive in a beautiful rural village? Tragically, it's never about the setting and the scenery. It's the people that make a place and an atmosphere. I shall always be grateful for Grandpa's warmth and love, which I believe kept me alive through the coldness and cruelty of the nights when the rituals happened.

> *Books have been written on how satanic rituals are performed and recognised. For a long time I thought that what happened to me must be OK because it didn't follow the "official" patterns. After years of ministering to others, I now see that the enemy has fairly simple ways of leading people astray, but how they work those out in practice can vary. The key is looking for his footprint and character, which are totally against the love and goodness of God. I have grown to see the truth that Satan is not only the "accuser of [the] brethren"[1], but also the accuser of God to the brethren, for such was the pattern of all I suffered as a child.*
>
> *I won't go into detail, but I do want to write enough to help others find hope and freedom if they are trapped in his cruel holds and deceptions. I want to bring light and hope to any of you who are lost in darkness and hopelessness. Believe me, I've been there over and over again.*

The satanic rituals involved perverse cruelty to children. Initially, my sister was "given" to Gran. My mother had no say in the matter. Abandoned and abused at a tender age, Mum was vulnerable to manipulation, control, and deception.

But when Annabella was just over three years old, she was knocked over by a motorbike whilst crossing a road in Gran's care. The family thought my sister had died, but her life was saved, and she became even more my mother's "special princess". Gran repented of all she had done to my sister, who was then left to my mum to treat as she wished. Both Mum and Dad struggled with guilt and anger over all that had happened to Annabella, and she became a very pampered child.

---

[1] Revelation 12:10 (KJV)

I was born six months before Annabella's accident. Given the importance of family line, my arrival as a girl was a catastrophe and I was called the "spare child" from a very early age. My *raison d'être* came when Annabella was in hospital. Gran's fear and superstition increased, so the enemy had a tighter grip. She was "given" me, the spare child, to replace Annabella. The whole village, shocked by Annabella's accident, leaped on the provision of another child. My destiny was to be trained to take over Gran's powers when she died. There, but for God's amazing grace, is where I would have been today, used in destroying countless lives. Praise God, He had other plans. His power and love surpass anything the enemy can throw at us. He is the God who seeks us out and rescues us from the "valley of the shadow"[2].

---

[2] Psalm 23:4

2

Training begins

It was easy to take me to rituals before I was five years old. Mum and Dad spent a lot of time living with Gran, even though they had a home of their own. Mum had nowhere else to go and very little say in any matter. She was such a strong and intelligent woman; it was a tragedy to see how her emotional damage had left her insecure and helpless, but it's the weak and injured the enemy seeks to influence. Maybe that's why Jesus' mandate is so clearly to the hurting, the sinners, and the oppressed. Of course it is – what a Saviour!

So from the age of six months to five years I was "trained" – trained to ignore my conscience and do only what was demanded of me in rituals and other training times. The abuse was physical, sexual, and emotional – and deeply painful and confusing, particularly as family and trusted friends were responsible for it. The lie fed to me was that the pain would go if I did as the adults told me. This involved oaths and agreements, and obscene practices like drinking blood, being covered in urine and faeces, cutting, and sexual abuse, including the pushing of rods into my body. At the end of many rituals I was shut in a dark box, room, or coffin, and told to call on "Grandpa's God" for help. God never seemed to come, but the adults who shut me in did come, eventually, to let me out. Their aim was to make me trust them, not God, as my real saviour.

At other times, I saw a man, who I was told was my father, shut in a coffin and upside down on a cross. Sometimes they did this to me too, so I would know what Dad was suffering. The only way to save Dad, or myself, was to do as they said or to let them do as they pleased with my body.

You may ask, as I have, how anybody could do these things to a child. What I have described is a brief glimpse of what was repeated practice. It all happened in a frenzy of noise and chanting in dark, secret places. I was often drugged with a handkerchief of chloroform, so my memories of faces can be hazy. In my healing, I have had to revisit memory upon memory, and let Jesus in to heal, which He has done marvellously.

Our bodies hold memories as well as our minds. Often a body sensation lingers longer than a thought, or else it triggers the thought. In ritual abuse all these aspects of human response are used to lock agreements, threats, oaths, and bondage into the body and mind of a child in the hope they'll never get free. Those who aren't saved, healed, and blessed as I have been, live on in the deception and fear wrought through these early ritual activities. They can end up as very dangerous, difficult people, or locked up in prison or a mental hospital. The fact that I have been miraculously saved from this is the reason I have been encouraged to write my story; I want others who have been trapped like me to know there is a way out.

My "training" was intense from the ages of one to five. I was gifted with insight into others' lives and spirits, which is why Gran and the village particularly wanted to train me. One ritual involved adults bowing down to me as a queen. It had horrible sexual content, but something in me loved the attention and affirmation. As a very emotionally-deprived child, affirmation and attention felt like a matter of life and death to me. This was very hard to let go when I was going through healing and release. In the same way, a child's desire for parental love and approval is used to push the child into things he or she would never want to do or experience, such as pain, abuse, and hurting others. That's why memories of Dad in a coffin or being abused or hurt on a cross pushed me into doing whatever he or any adult ever told me to do. I was desperate to save him and felt very responsible for him. I was also threatened with never-ending illness and torment and pain for me and my family if I ever left the ritual circle. Breaking free took a lot of time and courage and strong, patient love from others, and the wonderful healing and freeing truth of Jesus: the way, the truth and the life.

By the time I was five I had psychic gifting. I "knew" when people were ill, or going to die, and this was very frightening. One of the indications of demonic bondage is that it breeds fear, which forces you into doing the horrible things the enemy feeds into your mind. This causes constant misery and torment. My testimony is that, in sharpest contrast, Jesus brings love, joy and peace when we believe and obey Him.

3

Move to Lorrisford

As my night-time abuse continued, my father was ambitious for a headship and an opportunity presented itself in Lorrisford, to which we then moved. We returned to Granville House every holiday and often at weekends. Gran also visited Lorrisford so, sadly, my "training" continued.

In our new home, I was thrust into longer times with my mother. Up to this point she had been able to leave me with Gran or "farm me out to other women who 'liked' babies!" In later years she was shamelessly blunt, telling me she was forced into pregnancy because the family needed a boy to carry on its name. She was ill and required bed rest, and told me how she would think of every possible way to end the pregnancy. Confused and damaged by her abandonment in the children's home, she learned to hate at an early age and struggled with many emotional problems, which were often directed at me.

Mum felt she saved my life by sending me to be cared for by other women. Her reasons were, "I couldn't stand you," "I would have killed you if I'd had to be with you," and, "I tried to get rid of you in several ways but, damn you, you lived!"

So our times together in Lorrisford were fraught. To add insult to injury, Mum conceived again and miscarried. She blamed me for damaging her inside because I was born too fast. She was convinced the child she lost was the required and much desired boy.

Aged two to four, I knew her wrath, but I didn't understand it. It was later in life that she explained things to me. To give glory where it belongs, God helped me to keep relating to Mum and, three months before she died, He visited her in a miraculous way. Those last three months were precious times of sharing the joy of knowing Him, reading John 14, and praying with and for her. She was a gentle soul. Her whole life had been full of fear and all she came to want was to go and be at peace with the Jesus who visited her in her hospital room. I was thirty-three years old when she died. Mum had terminal cancer, but in those last three months she sought to care for me. She reassured me she'd be in a great place in heaven. She saved fruit gums in her drawer for me to eat when I visited, and she begged me to share her hospital cup of tea, wishing aloud she could boil a kettle for me. Her sweetest words to me were, "You need a mother!"

For her to say that was a miracle. It was real evidence of the change God can bring to a heart and life, but it created a dilemma. I loved the changes in her, but I had gone through thirty-two years of hatred, loneliness, and longing, always being the butt of her pain and anger. She had never protected me from Dad, Gran, and the rituals. When I'd been ill and lost my first child, Mum had been angry that I wasn't giving *her* the care she needed. From an early age, she'd asked me to keep quiet about all my wants and achievements in case Annabella got jealous. This had given my sister full rein to rule the house. It took very little from me to throw my sister into screaming hysterics. In recent years Annabella has told me how she hated even the sight of me, but in time, she too has come to be a follower of Jesus. He restores all things.

> *He does restore all things, but that process can take time. I think it's because He values the depth of our nature and knows us so well. My dream of a mum came true, but I still had a lifetime of grief, rejection, verbal, and physical cruelty, and all sorts of abuse to bring to Jesus for healing. I needed His love to heal so I could forgive and receive His truth.*
>
> *This healing aspect of my life's journey now forms the basis of Bespoke³, a wonderful ministry God has opened for my husband and me to work in together. No matter what our history, God can heal. No matter what lies we may have learned to believe, Jesus' truth can set us free and give us new paths to walk in. No matter what cruelty has hurt us, Jesus can meet us in our painful memories and transform them to places of joy and*

³ *www.bespokepollards.com*

healing. Wherever there is pain and wrong, the enemy likes to set up a stronghold, but no stronghold is too great for Jesus to dismantle.

As a trained counsellor and therapist, I've learned of the effects of parental neglect and cruelty and what we suffer as children. Many have marvelled that I've never been admitted to a mental hospital, and that I function at all as an adult. My joy and testimony is that nothing is impossible for God. All through my early childhood horrors, there was somehow a thread of God's saving grace. Through Grandpa, and in later life through both secular therapy and ministry, I have been able to grow in faith and freedom to live a full life. I hope my life has been and always will be a testimony to God's wonderful gift to us in Jesus.

4

Life in the village improves

When I was four, life took a brief turn for the better during a long holiday at Granville House. I still remember, vividly, the place and the time it changed. Grandpa had a bog garden. He built concrete troughs around the edges and in the centre, though in memories of this particular morning I am more aware of squatting on a sloping rockery near the entrance. All that happened to me in the night horrors deeply affected my self-esteem and I found it hard to play or be a happy child. I had to learn to cover my mood much more as the years went on. On this day, I was crouched, miserable, and cold on the rockery, when Grandpa walked by. He asked me questions: "What's wrong? What's been happening?" My training ensured I didn't say a word, but I couldn't stop the tears falling as I responded to each question with, "Nothing."

I clearly presented him with a dilemma because later that day I witnessed a row between Grandpa and my father and that night I was moved into the beautiful oak-panelled lounge. Up to this point I had slept in my parents' room, in what was called "the chair bed". I remember going to sleep in that bed but have no memory of ever waking up in it. Sometimes I was left out in the garden very early in the morning, and only called in for breakfast when Grandpa was around. When he wasn't, my being fed depended on how much "favour" I'd earned with Gran and the household.

When I was very little, the chair bed was fine. I was small as a child (I think it is now known as "failure to thrive"), but as I grew bigger I could no longer stretch out on the bed, and being forced to curl up was painful. I'd be punished for complaining. Grandpa knew none of this as he slept in the shed.

When Dad and Grandpa rowed I thought it was about the bed, because the oak-panelled lounge housed a bed settee which was wonderfully long for me. I remember Gran giving me a sheet to put on it (quite hard when you're four!). She was very cross, so I knew something had been said.

I had mixed feelings about the oak-panelled room. Somehow, I was very conscious that Gran's bedroom was directly above me. The stairs were outside the lounge and the back porch was next to its door. As I climbed onto my new bed I was terrified. I found myself listening for Gran's footsteps and realised that the porch door was the one they used to take me out of the house in the middle of the night. It hadn't been so clear before because I was usually half asleep. That first night I searched for a chair or broom that might block the high door handle from opening. My stress grew because the furniture was hard to move and there was no broom. (For anyone who needs to know, though I sincerely hope you don't, an inverted broom at the right angle can make a wonderful door stop. I've often used that in places where I've known there was danger. It annoys people on the outside, but that's far easier to overcome than the alternative.)

That night then turned into something really special. I found a key on the windowsill which I suspect Grandpa had left for me. It fitted the door lock. I'd always been forbidden to lock myself in anywhere, but this night I felt brave, or desperate, and I locked the door. It created havoc outside. Late in the night I heard Dad and Gran shouting at me, but they were firmly locked in the hallway. They tried the serving hatch in the kitchen, but I'd fastened the bolt on that as well. Not bad for a four-year-old! I learned to be creative and resourceful at an early age.

> Something we love to do for people is to pray what we call "original design". Others call it spiritual DNA, or kingdom blueprint. It's based on Psalm 139 and Ephesians 2. The truth behind it is that God created us "before the foundation of the world"[4] and in our mother's womb He formed our inward parts. He has good works for us to walk in; every day ordained for us is written in his book. One of our passions is to help people

---

[4] John 17:24

encounter the God they've never known and live the difference.
That first encounter with God never fails to be miraculous. If the
person is willing, we pray and ask God how He made them in
His original plan before life messed things up and tried to rob
them of their godly character and gifting. What we hear from
God never ceases to amaze the person and their friends. In my
own original design there is much about being a runner after
God, a woman of the Word, a mother, loving, nurturing and
creative. There's a lot more, but the main characteristics, aged
four, were creativity and resourcefulness. I'm also a "warrior",
but fighting caused me problems as a child!

Grandpa, now on the alert, picked up Dad and Gran's anger about
my first night in the oak-panelled room. He didn't make a fuss, or have
an argument. I love recalling his ability to combine peace and authority.
It makes me want to chuckle and weep at the same time – weep because
the situation was so sad, but chuckle that this gentle old man, who was
generally despised and ignored, could cause everyone to scurry and
submit with a few simple words. There is real power in simplicity.
Grandpa didn't lay down the law very often, but when he did no one
argued. In fact, no one said a word. They didn't even complain.

"I'm moving in," was his simple announcement. No one questioned
him. Everyone discussed his reasons – too cold, hard to breathe – but I
knew. In my heart of hearts, I'm sure it was for me. He took me on one
side and said, "Don't worry, love. Lock the door and be assured, I'm
sleeping in the dining room just next door."

I was safely locked in so no one came near me and Grandpa had the
key. He organised an old china chamber pot for me so I didn't have to
go upstairs. He helped me empty it discreetly. I think he was also
checking that my bleeding and discharges were healing up. I began to
blossom from peaceful nights of real sleep, safety, and security. All this
time my faith in God was growing under Grandpa's delightful
instruction through flowers, animals, games, walks, and woodwork. To
this day I still feel close to God in the outdoors and with animals. I also
saw Grandpa's beautiful faith in action. By now he was quite hard of
hearing so when he prayed aloud I could hear him in my lounge. He
chatted to God just like Moses. God talked to Moses "as a man talks to

his friend"[5]. Jesus calls us friends and that's what Grandpa modelled for me. It was truly a taste of heaven having him in the house, but life takes turns and it took another all too soon.

> *It's a while since I've written. Interestingly, that's another legacy from my past. I'm over sixty years old now. That's a miracle in itself. I survived and I'm not in a mental institution. That's not our God though, is it? With Him we do more than survive. He rescues us out of the valley of the shadow and gives us double honour for our shame and a life which is truly abundant.*
>
> *The human body can heal amazingly. That's why I loved surgical nursing. Doctors would chop around in someone's body and everything would heal better than it was before. That's what's happened for me. My body was seriously damaged by what happened to me as a child, and I've had over sixteen surgical operations, most of them major, and five of them to heal cancer. Much of the healing I've had has been more than the doctors could have expected. That's God's loving intervention. The legacy is that I seem to pick up a lot of viruses in certain seasons of life. Two dear friends were recently killed in a car accident, and then my father died. On the day we buried him, my mother-in-law also died. As my doctor said, "Even though you know how to cope as a trained counsellor," – which I now am – "it doesn't mean that life doesn't affect you." That's true, but maybe I feel things more deeply. My griefs are what therapists call "complex griefs". I can become very anxious and afraid if I feel weak or under the weather. The things that go wrong with my body often remind me of many of my childhood traumas. That's my struggle and my sadness. I'm increasingly learning to handle the deep feelings of fear, pain, and rejection, but what happened to me should never happen to anybody. Thank God for the release of forgiveness and that He knows how to comfort us because He has shared our sufferings on the cross – "the cross, the wonderful cross of Jesus". For me it's the power of this resurrection life that spurs me on to know Him more and more intimately. So when I'm ill I seek to push into*

---

[5] Exodus 33:11

Him with my struggles and questions, tears and pain. He never fails to surprise me with His specific, intensely personal love and comfort. I now enjoy ministering to others who are suffering in the myriad of ways life throws at us. God meets them too, just as and when they need it, with what Psalm 46:1 calls "a very present and well-proved help in trouble" (AMP).

5

Gran dies

Because I was a "gifted" child, in a spiritual sense, around 1956 my ritual training intensified. It is said that psychics are simply spiritually gifted people using unhelpful sources for their knowledge and leading.

I hated having insight into when people were ill and which parts of their body were diseased. I also had a sense when someone might die. If they did die, I was filled with fear that somehow it was my fault. The only way I could handle such fear at such a young age was to use my ritual training much more intensely. Pain in parts of my body would push me further into these practices because they eased the discomfort.

When I received prayer for release from this, forty-five years later, I realised how the villagers had used pain and abuse to push me into using ritual training as a way of coping with life. A complex web of agreements and oaths is enforced by fearful scenes and much physical, sexual, and emotional abuse. Praise God for His life within me and His loving servants and gentle Holy Spirit! These wonders have made possible a total unravelling of all that had sought to keep me trapped in fear, misery, and torment.

Dad always wanted to return to his country home so he could be immersed in the village activities, and at this time an opportunity arose for him to become a head teacher at Rushford and he took it. He had hoped for a post in the same county as his home village and was sad to leave his beloved north for another city, but the draw of a brand-new school and headship was strong.

We moved to Rushford just before the Easter school holidays, when my sister spent a week in Dawley with my aunt, uncle, and two cousins. She sailed confidently through her time away. My aunt and family came to Rushford for a day to bring Annabella home. At some point during that day they started to taunt me, mocking everything I did; I'm not sure why. I still wonder if it was a planned or calculated attack. Their repeated comment was, "Annabella can do that so much better than you." Whatever the reason, their mockery was relentless. I was already feeling miserable when someone suggested I should try a week away with them in the summer. It wasn't so much an invitation as a challenge: "You wouldn't be able to do a week away, but Annabella can." Something rose in me – probably my fighting spirit, the warrior part of my original design. I decided to take up the offer. Everyone was surprised and my father was angry. I was to learn never to challenge him in future. Pulling me to one side, he said, "You are stepping outside my jurisdiction, making a decision outside my advice. If you find you can't manage this, you need to know I will not help you. Disobedience puts you outside my protection." In later years, he reiterated this sort of warning as, "Be this on your own head," or, "You're on your own with this one."

A few months later, Gran died from bowel cancer. I discovered that she had been ill for several months and later understood why my training had intensified – to prepare me to take over from her!

At the time, I hoped that the horrors of the rituals would end with Gran's death as we'd already moved away from the village. However, the enemy weaves networks of people to keep us trapped. My dad was utterly bound to the village. He and Mum were teachers, so every holiday and many weekends found us back in the north.

> *I've really struggled to start writing today. When I began this book, I found a thirty-minute slot to pray and start writing was quite a release and often exciting. As I've approached the period when I was five to nine years old I've been increasingly reluctant to put pen to paper. This was the time I began to "lose" Grandpa.*

What Dad hadn't anticipated with his change of job was that his mother would die only three months into his headship. Grief is strange and my family was not good at handling it. It isn't just about the death of a person. Stress analysis categorises "moving house", "changing your job", and even "going on holiday" as sources of grief or loss. Bereavement can also bring up sadness and anger linked with other losses – in Dad's case, that of his siblings. Their loss had been the impetus that led Gran and the village into the occult. I believe that Dad was confused at this time. Gran's "spirituality" was diametrically opposed to Grandpa's. Perhaps this is why Dad and Mum even tried church when we first reached Rushford. I went with them, but ritual training causes problems in a Christian setting, and I remember hating communion. I would feel intensely angry and often had pain in embarrassing parts of my body. I also struggled because Dad would shake and begin to swear quietly as the bread and wine were being blessed. Eventually I gave up church and later on my parents followed suit. They didn't feel at home there.

> *So here I am, writing again. I've been troubled by the darkness and sadness in me and over me as I reach this place in my story. My therapeutic training and experience tell me I'm simply feeling the sadness of the five-to-nine-year-old. One of the questions I often ask clients who have a feeling that doesn't seem to fit their current circumstances is, "How old do you feel when you have this feeling?" It's a helpful way to access unresolved memories from the past and to identify where the emotions from that time have been buried. So, "Physician, heal yourself!"[6] When I ask myself how old I feel in the darkness and sadness I'm experiencing now, my answer is five years old and sometimes six.*

It was at this point in my life that I was first given antidepressants or tranquilisers. According to my parents, I suddenly became very difficult. I refused to go to music lessons and struggled to go to school. I'd already gained a distinction in my Grade One piano exam, so my parents were angry that I didn't want to continue, and they forced me to. I was small and afraid enough to be manhandled into the car and into the music teacher's house. She was very kind and gentle so I would gain confidence to play my pieces despite the tears that flowed. Whichever parent had forced me there was firmly told to sit in another room; I love Mrs Hartman for that.

---

[6] Luke 4:23 (AMP)

I was also forced to go to the dentist. I'd been before, but now something uncomfortable happened deep inside me when the kind gentleman stood over me. I lashed out and screamed inconsolably. He tried his hardest to speak kindly and make up counting games, but I couldn't cooperate. My parents were furious and desperate. Despite their reluctance to have a second daughter, they had started taking more interest since my intelligence and charm won them attention, especially in their world of education. Dad was making his way in his brand-new school and I was a good advert for him as what he called "a model child". My success made him look and feel good as a parent and educator.

So what had happened to bring about such a change in me?

6

The horrendous week

The time eventually came for my week in Dawley with my aunt and her family. Despite the fact that Dad had told me that my disobedience would put me outside his protection, I wanted to believe that he really did care, whatever he might say. I told myself that if I couldn't cope, my parents would surely come to my aid. They were due to visit Grandpa anyway, and were on holiday, so all they needed to do was come a day or two early.

I'll never know if it was a plan set up between the relatives, or what really happened. All I know is I was trapped at my aunt's for a whole week, and my uncle was extremely abusive. He was an osteopath and had a surgery with a doctor's couch in it. My female cousins saw him lure me in there early in the week and screamed to me to run away before he closed the door. He still insisted on bathing me at night and found other ways to do appalling things to my tiny body. One night I locked myself in the toilet. It had a big key and Grandpa had taught me how to use them to keep safe. My uncle came to the door and was very angry to find himself locked out. I was terrified. I don't know how they got me out; I think he removed the lock in the end. By that time, I'd fallen asleep on the toilet floor. My aunt was part of an all-female ritual circle and I find I'm still tense at times in a group of women. I know now this is an archaic memory, but the cruelty of her group left me seriously scarred. Jesus has brought great healing, so when the memory recurs I can move to His tenderness and compassion and reassure myself that "this" is not "that".

My parents phoned daily, and my aunt stood over me at every call. I plucked up the courage to beg to go home early but my parents refused my tearful request every time. The day to move on to Grandpa's arrived. I was excited to see my family again and I thought they'd be pleased to see me. Dad gathered my aunt, uncle, and cousins and my mum and sister in the large hallway. I thought we were simply going to say goodbye, but I was so mistaken. This gathering still haunts me; its effect has been pivotal in my life. With the whole family gathered, my father pointed to me and said, "This child has disgraced her whole family. She has dishonoured her aunt and uncle and despised their generous hospitality. Instead of gratitude she has insisted on complaining about them daily. From this moment on she is disowned from this family and no one is to speak to her for three weeks." I was stunned by his words and the authority in his voice. I felt sentenced.

From that moment on, nothing was said to me. Everyone hugged and said goodbye to each other, but I was totally ignored.

Several times I'd heard both my parents and Gran refer to me as "the spare child". Remember, after Annabella, a son had been required to carry on the family name, and when I arrived instead of a son my mother began to hate me. I was kept alive because I could replace my sister in the rituals after her road accident. She was alive and well, but my parents' guilt at the accident made her their "princess" for life. Gran had been with Annabella at the accident and felt extremely responsible, so she repented of all she had done to her in rituals and was relieved to have me to replace her. This gave my mother a sense of satisfaction; she had finally managed to do something right for Gran and the village to counter some of the disgrace of failing to produce a son. So I had already been taught to see myself as the spare child. This Dawley experience and its miserable ending sealed this identity. A spare child has no voice, no rights, and is only fit to be used by others. To a child like me, being useful was vital to staying alive. This horrendous week bound me to my father more strongly than ever.

This was the root of my behaviour changes and intense sadness aged five to nine. I believe I could have been suicidal at an early age had it not been for the grace of God and my hero, Grandpa.

> *At the moment, I feel anxious every day until I've written for thirty minutes. If I didn't allocate that time and seek to be faithful to keep to my decision, I would definitely stop writing*

this book. This is a painful process. Even today I have to battle a deep depression and fear of rejection, especially if I am unwell or unable to do what someone wants. I know how to handle depression. I am a trained therapist and counsellor, but that doesn't prevent pain and fear from rising.

One way I cope and help others to do the same is to "let the child speak". I take the role of a loving adult and encourage my "inner child" to talk to me. Writing with my left hand helps her to do so; I'm right-handed, so using my non-dominant hand and a pencil puts me back into the place of a child with difficulties in expressing and communicating. Sometimes I write back from my adult self. This is an interim step to going straight to Jesus for His response. My child didn't know Jesus for herself. Her attachment to Him was through Grandpa. Isn't that why parents and adults are given to us? They are to love, nurture, build us up, and teach us all about His love for us. By letting my adult reply, I receive or access some of the nurture I was so badly lacking. Often, I'll weep for myself. In fact, that's a real reaction. I remember Grandpa holding back the tears when he realised what was happening to me. Sometimes the two-way writing is enough, but generally I love to ask God for His response. He amazes me with His sensitivity and His knowledge of exactly what I need to hear or feel from Him. I've encouraged many people to work in this manner. It is witnessing God's unique response to each child of His that thrills my husband and me in our ministry together.

7

New friends

It was to Grandpa's house that we were travelling after my aunt's house. God is so good. Many of the people who have offered me love, care, and ministry have exclaimed, "Thank God for Grandpa!" and I echo that. Grandpa quickly spotted that something was very wrong when we arrived at his house and immediately questioned my father. Mum and Annabella stayed quiet in the background. Dad repeated his edict that no one was to speak to me and his accusations of dishonour, although he didn't mention disowning me. I think he'd seen Grandpa's rising anger and indignation. There was a strange moment of silence – the sort that hangs in the air and you know something is about to burst. Grandpa was trembling; Dad was speechless; Mum and Annabella retreated. Calmly and with authority, Grandpa called them back. He gathered the whole family and told them firmly that not speaking to me was cruel and ridiculous and not allowed in his house.

I felt blessed, protected, and released from my sentence – but not completely. The pain of that week was severe. The wounds of being accused and disowned by the family I always hoped would rescue me were unbearable. Great damage had been done.

Grandpa's protection was wonderful, but it didn't fully clear the pain and tension between me and the rest of my family. The word "disowned" haunted me. I was safe with Grandpa, but at the end of a stay I always had to leave and go back to school and life in Rushford.

That holiday at Grandpa's was the beginning of my quest for new friends. On trips to fetch milk from the local farm, I'd made a friend called Mr Galloway. He was a lovely old farmer, and one of Grandpa's best friends. He let me ride a pig once, which he called Helen, which at the time I found flattering!

He used to keep piglets. I liked them as friends, but they had needle-like teeth and I didn't like their smelly sty. The calves were kinder and the lambs were cute. Calves were fun to train to drink from a bucket, and I was taught to let them suck my fingers and lower my hand into the milk. The idea was to remove my hand once the calf was sucking milk. Once or twice, however, the calf hung on with its teeth. I decided calves weren't such good friends. Not many lambs needed bottle-feeds, which I enjoyed. The way these animals grew up and became less friendly was a constant struggle for me.

I liked the farm kittens, but they were half wild and would hurt and even spit at me as they grew older. One of my favourite friends was Winnie, who purred a lot. She wasn't very pretty, but then neither was I, so we had a real bond. She also spent hours outside – another point in common. She was warm and let me stroke her, but I could never pick her up. We had a good friendship so long as I kept my boundaries. Many a scratch or bite taught me those. We got along well until one day I watched her catch a mouse. She didn't just kill it; she kept hurting it, then letting it run away. It seemed as if she was loving it and just playing, but then she'd hurt it again. I'm sure the poor mouse was confused and terrified. He kept thinking his pain and torment were over and then they would start again.

I identified so strongly with the mouse. He seemed to be living out before my eyes the pain and fear and confusion I so frequently experienced. Winnie was now a problem to me. Adults told me the mouse would die so it would be OK, and that it was natural for cats to act in that way. Neither of these comments brought me the reassurance I needed. Even Grandpa said the same and that hurt me, though I'd never say. I could never explain even to him why I felt so wretched. I don't think I knew why. I was too young and had always been forbidden to speak about what happened to me in the night rituals.

I was utterly lonely and miserable. The family only spoke to me when they had to and Grandpa spent a lot of time in bed or in his cabin. I didn't know how unwell he was, and I felt abandoned. So I started to build friends for myself – friends I could talk to, love, and rely on to be there. I built a toy horse and found him really helpful. I was worried he'd be lonely when I had to go back to Rushford, so I built him two more friends.

They lived in Grandpa's old summerhouse. Each had a stall, a straw bed and plenty of food and water. They were made of wood with woollen manes and tails. With a rug on, I believed no one would know they weren't real horses.

> *Some more legacy. I've been ill again. Since Dad died more memories have surfaced. The stress of these has rendered me open to infection and a recent resurgence of shingles.*

These horses grew to be my best friends, but there was always something lacking. I couldn't sit on them and they were hard and didn't move. For a while I employed a small wall with a raised end as my riding pony, and made a bridle and saddle with stirrups so I could practise rising trot. I was saddened when I overheard Grandpa say to my parents, "That child spends too much time on her own." I'd taken him to see my horses and thought he was impressed with the hours I'd spent creating these friends. Even with me his response had been somewhat subdued, but, true to his beautiful nature, Grandpa responded to the love he noticed I had for animals and, whilst on holiday by the sea, introduced me to the donkeys on the beach. I began to spend blissful days working with the donkey man. This progressed to my learning to ride in Rushford. I had pocket money once every two weeks, which I used for my lessons. I soon began to work at the stables, which gained me extra rides, especially bareback trips to the night grazing paddock.

By the age of nine I was regularly out of the house and at the stables for two days a week. It was still hard making friends because we were back in the village of Granville every school holiday and at weekends when Grandpa was in hospital. The frequency of those weekends increased as his heart condition grew more severe. Children can be cruel, and the children around me soon picked up on my weaknesses and sensitivities, and enjoyed playing on them. Many times, they would agree together to perform an activity without me and even refused to speak to me. Rejection, isolation, and silence were three of my worst nightmares. These could be sad days, but the horses remained faithful, and always seemed pleased to see me.

Grandpa arranged riding for me in a nearby village with the daughter of a farming family called the Wests. Emily West was delightful. She was two years younger than me, but quite mature and confident, probably due to her good experiences at boarding school. Her sister Samantha, however, was a different character altogether. She was five or six years older, and her school experience had been difficult. She now attended a private day school and was set on training to become a model. As two grubby pre-teenagers, we were not her favourite people, but she owned the nicest pony I'd ever known, so we had to keep on the best side of her as much as we could. The pony was called Rushing Water, or Rush for short. He was pretty, loving, and very fast. Samantha's parents said I was welcome to ride him whenever my family was at Granville.

Emily owned a tiny Shetland pony called Reggie. She loved him dearly and was very patient with him, although he was strong and very stubborn. If we rode out with Rush, Reggie was quite amenable, and Emily would generously ride him so I could enjoy Rush. We had some truly delightful times together. We even took the ponies swimming in the river. The northern countryside is breathtaking and I am eternally grateful to Grandpa, the Wests and Emily for many wonderful rides and blissful days on the farm. Grandpa loved to come out and say hello and feed the ponies, so we used to ride over to see him at his house. In my lonely, terrible days after ritual nights, I would relive our visits to the garden to encourage myself to keep living.

8

Rage released

One day it all got too much. It was a weekend and as Grandpa was seriously ill, we had come up to see him. Mr and Mrs West invited me to ride Rush. They did many things to cheer me up, as I think they realised how troubled I was. I walked the several miles to their farm in the late afternoon because I hadn't been allowed to go earlier; Grandpa hadn't been there to fight for me. The Wests said it was still fine to ride Rush and told me where to find him. I was so excited and desperate to have a break from the misery of Grandpa's illness and all that happened at Granville House when he wasn't there. I found Rush in his barn, had a cuddle with him, and was just on my way to find his tack when Samantha arrived. She simply stood there and said, "I don't want you to ride Rush today. You can take Reggie." I told her Reggie would be very difficult on his own but there was no reasoning or arguing. She'd hidden Rush's tack and left Reggie's so my choice was Reggie or nothing.

I went to find him. He'd not been in a barn, so needed a lot of cleaning up. Finally, he was saddled and we began our ride. I debated how far to go, but Reggie was behaving well so I risked the road route to Granville House. Halfway there I realised that we were unlikely to get back before dark so I decided to cross the field by the river and head back home to the farm. I was thanking God that Reggie was going so well; it really was a miracle. Dusk was falling but we were homeward bound. I was sure Reggie would trot home merrily. For reasons I will never know, halfway across the field he stood stock still. Nothing I did could persuade him to move. I got on and off several times, wondering if leading him would work, but discovering it didn't. In fact, as soon as I dismounted he simply pulled his head free to eat grass at the side of the track. I began to feel anxious about getting home before dark. Grandpa was ill, so no one would come to look for me and they'd be angry with me for being late to help with tea.

> *What happened next frightened and shamed me for decades. I'm now in my sixties and I only prayed this memory through a year ago. I met God wonderfully in the prayer and have spoken about this since on some teaching sessions. However, back to the field, Reggie, and the falling dusk.*

I dismounted and tried to persuade Reggie to move towards home. The more I pleaded, the firmer he planted his feet. I pulled and pushed him and then I lost all control. I began to kick him behind his girth. I stood at the side and held his reins and kicked and kicked and screamed. He didn't move at all. Rage is the only word I have to describe what I was feeling – uncontrollable rage. Somewhere in my kicking, Reggie let out a long breath and fell to the ground. I was sure he was dead. Now my tears began to roll, and I wailed, crying out to God, "Help me, help me! What have I done?" I lay down near Reggie and prayed loudly and desperately, "God if you're there, I'm so sorry, but please don't let him be dead."

Reggie gasped once or twice but still couldn't move. I was beside myself, but prayed all the more. Then he suddenly rolled off his side and on to his knees. He stayed there a while and I knelt to hug him and tell him how sorry I was. He nuzzled my arm which made me cry all the more. We stayed cuddling and nuzzling for a while, both kneeling in the middle of the vast field. Then Reggie rose to his feet and I pulled up big bundles of lush grass for him. I'm sure he smiled at me. He began to eat and I hugged him again and prayed, thanking God and asking that Reggie would have no injuries from the brutal kicking. Having felt him all over and groomed him with my bare hands I was happy he was uninjured. Dusk was really falling now so I prayed again. I prayed that Reggie would move and the light would hold. It took some courage to ask Reggie to move. I was scared of my despair if he didn't. Miraculously, he was now keen to go where I wanted. I was relieved and surprised but I daren't ride him. I was still afraid he may be injured, or at least bruised and tired. We ran together all the way to the road that led to the farm gate, and he seemed happier than I'd ever known. I

49

mounted at the bottom of the last lane, so no one would know that anything had happened. He trotted home merrily. I hastily settled him into his field, hugged him again and ran all the way back to Granville. I was in big trouble but I didn't retaliate at all. I was frightened of myself and felt so evil that I almost welcomed the punishments I received. It would need more than guilt and punishment to clear my shame.

> *I now realise my rage was probably a healthy response to my abnormal childhood experiences. When I prayed through this memory I sensed God's smile and reassurance that Reggie was unscarred by the experience. Instead, God's salvation was expressed through Reggie's rising up unscarred, and His forgiveness in the "love" Reggie demonstrated in response to my rage.*

Ever after that day, Reggie was a joy to ride, and Emily was in awe of his willing obedience when I was around to ride him.

> *All these years later God has finally helped free me of my shame and fear of myself. I owe Reggie a lot, but I owe God so much more! I've both forgiven and thanked Samantha for who she was and what she did, especially on that crucial day.*
>
> *They say that hindsight is a wonderful thing. We can learn a lot from our mistakes but the incident with Reggie didn't help me in that way. I was sure loving and caring for him had forged a new relationship, but I tried to avoid the memory of kicking him in my rage. Sadly, however, I couldn't block it out, and I remained afraid of myself. The rituals taught me that I was full of evil and my parents often called me a devil. When my mother took me to her physiotherapy class aged just two years old she asked people not to speak to me because I was uncontrollable and evil. The other patients objected but Mum was adamant. In some ways, she had a point: I was prone to tantrums and hysterical outbursts. Now I realise that this was out of frustration with her and strong, confused reactions to abuse.*
>
> *Names and labels, even if said in jest, can have a profound effect on a child. In my work with young people, and even older ones, the pain of negative beliefs about themselves is all too real. It is destructive. We call these beliefs False Identity Statements. They are not how God intended us to view ourselves.*

During ministry, we like to catch the negative things people say about themselves, knock off the enemy's hold, and ask God for His replacement truth. Where couples are receiving ministry together, it's beautiful to have them read or pray Godly Identity Statements over each other. For single people, Steve and I will pray over them and sometimes record the prayers so they can hear the statements over and over again. Neuroscience says it takes forty days to make a new pathway in the brain. Forty days of listening to this new identity can transform a person's life forever.

9

Darkness increases

After my outburst of rage at Reggie, I saw myself as a carrier of real evil and someone capable of murder. Meanwhile, my parents were unhappy in Rushford and Annabella was increasingly demanding. She wasn't at all happy if things didn't go her way, and grammar school was a struggle for her.

My mother told me stories about her experiences in children's homes. My father often told me about the death of his siblings and his mother's sadness. I'm sure they were grieving and depressed. They also felt extremely guilty about Annabella's accident and, in the absence of any psychological help, life became torture for them and for me. They had struggled with my years of depression and agoraphobia, but had been angry and abusive in response, rather than understanding. In their eyes, I was gifted with brains and health and so owed it to them to be a model child and school pupil. Their reputation as a headmaster (my father) and teacher (my mother) was all important.

The riding stables helped to cheer me a great deal. Working there also kept me out of the house at weekends. I found ways of barring my bedroom door, so sleep was possible in Rushford and abuse couldn't happen.

Grandpa's health, however, was deteriorating and just before my tenth birthday he suffered a severe heart attack. We visited him every weekend, first in hospital and then for at least six weeks in a convalescent home. One day he was taken ill during our visit. He became very pale and unable to recognise us. Nurses came to help, and he recovered to live for another seven years. That day, however, the likelihood of losing him was all too real. I was so troubled within myself that I'd only focused on getting through each day, achieving as much as I could for my parents, and upsetting them as little as possible. The bigger picture hadn't entered my head.

We were allowed back to Grandpa's bedside and he seemed himself again, but I noticed he was weak and breathless. Anger rose inside me. I was shocked and afraid, dizzy and faint. The hospital ward had double glass doors which opened on to a field fringed by woodland. Without a word to anyone I made for the open air and ran. When I reached the woodland, I shook and screamed and wailed.

This kind of reaction overtook me frequently during the depressions I suffered later at university and in my adult life.

As the emotions rose, voices began to chant, "He's going to die; all you'll have is us. You have no choice but to do as we say." They said much more that I won't recall. This was the first time the ritual training and suffering had affected me so clearly in the cold light of day. From that day, this sort of mental torment increased.

I was sad and confused. I felt anger and hatred towards Grandpa, but that wasn't how I *really* felt – it felt like something apart from me. A new depression set in that day. I didn't want to burden my parents so I struggled to behave and do well at school. When Grandpa came home I was glad, but the threatening voices insisted he would die. I was afraid I could cause his death and was saddened by the new hatred that arose in me, especially when Grandpa talked about God.

I spent my tenth birthday in Rushford. My family were all very sad and I was miserable. No one wanted to celebrate my birthday. "Damn you, you lived," echoed in my head from my mother's stories about my birth and early years. I firmly believed I was only worthy of food and shelter if I served my family in every way they wanted. My service was clearly not working well on the eve of my birthday as they were all so unhappy. I felt evil for being alive, but I was too scared to die. The torment in my head was growing worse and I was still struggling with that inexplicable hatred of God and Grandpa.

On the day of my birthday I decided to go out, and walked the streets of Rushford trying to pray. That led to my decision to buy presents for my family to thank them for keeping me alive. The only shop still open was a local chemist. I found it hard to choose presents that would please them so I asked for the chemist's help. He seemed distressed when I told him why I wanted to buy presents for my family. His concern confused me and I insisted that what I was doing was right and essential.

I can't remember what I bought; I can't remember their response. I think they were pleased and had a sense that they deserved their gifts, but it didn't make things better. I knew I was doing badly at school and wondered if that explained their lack of enthusiasm. I also knew that barring my door at night angered my father. Mum and Annabella accepted my explanation that I was frightened of witches and intruders. The truth was I didn't want Dad coming in because of what he used to do to me. I couldn't tell them that. Dad would call Mum neurotic and say I was highly strung, but he knew the real reason.

10

Pinpricks of light

After this unhappy birthday, I searched and prayed for help in school. In my last year at primary school I had a wonderful teacher who realised something was very wrong with me. She talked to my parents and they simply expressed their anger and despair. Unperturbed, Mrs Knightley persisted in befriending me. She worked closely with the head teacher and they both invited me to their homes for tea. The head was wise and invited my parents as well, which was easy because Dad was a colleague and Mum and the head teacher's wife were teachers. When we visited, the head and his wife would praise me, play games, and give me lots of time and attention. My parents couldn't complain.

One day Mrs Knightley asked me to read a Bible passage. It was David's lament over Saul and Jonathan. I was deeply touched by David's expression of grief. Mrs Knightley was so impressed by the way I read that she recorded me reading it again and asked me to read the passage in the school assembly. A recording was sent to my parents who were excited by my school's pride in my talent.

When I read Scripture aloud the tormenting voices ceased in my head. I felt a peace like I had used to feel with Grandpa. I took to reading Scripture aloud whenever I could, and the school encouraged me.

I wrote a poem about the Israelites wanting a king and took it to Mrs Knightley, who was impressed. The head was too, and I was put on the stage in assembly again. With this discovery of peace, and devoted attention and encouragement, I began to blossom at school.

This pleased my parents and my depression lifted. I passed my 11+ with flying colours and was proud to gain a place at grammar school. My father loved the attention I brought him as a bright child, well-mannered and well-trained in serving. With my work at the stables my body grew strong and I pleased school and parents with my growing sporting prowess.

It's two or three weeks since I've written. I've been ill again and also working very hard. That's not the whole story. Easter has just passed. This is a high season in the satanic ritual calendar. I don't follow it too closely, but my husband keeps an eye on it so he can increase his intercessory protection over us and our growing family. Right now, I am raw from struggles with recurring memories. I think it's been harder this year because Dad has just died. He prayed with Steve before his death. I have felt encouraged that he is now at peace with Jesus, so memories of the sad, hard times are confusing. Confusion keeps me away from the pain, but it's not the answer. Harbouring pain and denying its effects brings physical problems. I know I need to let the troubling Easter memories come to light so I can find healing. My vicar has helped me see the truth of what's going on for me at the moment. Rituals take Christian symbols like the cross or communion chalice and use them in counterfeit, evil ceremonies. When these have been connected with pain, abuse, and cruelty in childhood, they leave a deep and lasting impression. This Easter I wanted happy memories of Dad, but what has happened in the past doesn't change when someone dies.

What does cheer me is Grandpa's emphasis on Jesus' resurrection. He rose from the dead so we could have new life. The power that raised Him from the dead now lives in us as Christians. I love to celebrate this mystery. How it works will become clear when I'm in heaven. What thrills me now is knowing His presence in me and with me every single day, and seeing how His life in me and in others brings wonderful joy and transformation. Please don't get stuck on my pain as you read this book. My purpose in writing is to tell you about Jesus' power to redeem, and His amazing ability to save us from any situation.

So where do I go from here? We just celebrated our 35th wedding anniversary. Our wedding was hard for me but Steve loved it. I loved God being there and I loved my beautiful husband. As we said to our daughter and son-in-law, it just got better and better. That's how it is when we know Jesus; a pinprick of light breaks into our lives and grows brighter and brighter. The Bible describes it as the first light of dawn increasing until new day. Steve and I now have three wonderful children, married to lovely partners, six gorgeous grandchildren and a ministry and church which are an answer to our deepest prayers and desires.

I managed well at senior school for about two years. Being clever and sporty won me friends, and more approval at home. Spending weekends with the horses kept me happy and out of the house. But then the tormenting voices began to increase again. Disturbing things happened in and to my body. The worst was a clumsiness that often led to mockery from others. Several times I would run to the bus stop for the stables but something seemed to hit the back of my knees and I'd fall in the street. This was embarrassing, but more than that it was intimidating. Sexual things would torment me at night. Voices would threaten me that Grandpa was soon to die, so I would no longer be protected. I would soon be wholly "theirs".

My school headmistress met me sometimes as I was running to the bus stop. Once I fell right in front of her. She expressed concern and invited me to talk about my troubles but I never could. I tried to ease my fears of losing Grandpa by going to church, but that only increased my torment. The headmistress attended our church and invited me to sit near her, but I never did. Somehow her concern made me feel very guilty.

But then another pinprick of light came into these dark days.

11

God is real

One night, after I had decided to get confirmed, I prayed, "God, if you are real, please give me a pony on my 14th birthday." I prayed this every night. By saying it over and over again, I could quell the sexual spirits and hold off the tormenting voices. The confirmation service was meaningful and Grandpa bought me a tiny book called *A Companion to Communion*, which I still have.

> *I'm about to go off to a conference in London, followed by several days of intensive ministry to people in churches just outside the city. I love what we do there and the conference is one I've often wanted to attend but never previously booked in time. We will stay with our beloved son and other dear friends. You'd expect me to be excited, but I find myself full of increasing dread and near to tears. I hate packing. Aged over sixty, and travelling as we do, you'd think I could pack by now! I'm stressed because there's a tube strike. We have to walk a lot and we booked into a hotel near the conference centre.*
>
> *I've just spent some time in 1 Corinthians 13. A book I read yesterday suggested writing the chapter out in my own words. That's a familiar exercise that I love to do, so I've made a start. I realise I'm full of striving: it's not just about being a good speaker or using my skills well; it's about packing my case wisely, being able to sleep in strange places, able to keep up with young people when we walk, or being friendly, secure and not grumpy when I'm tired and surrounded by people.*

> *Writing to Papa God with my left hand I find my heart is stuck with five-year-old Helen who had the horrendous week of abuse at the hands of her aunt and uncle. I often go back to that place. After that week, I was plagued by fears of ever leaving home, of packing, of sleeping, and of being with strangers.*

When I was thirteen I tried going away again, on a drama workshop. Drama was something I could do well. I've since found it's a way of escape and expression for many troubled people. The time away was everything I feared, as I found I couldn't sleep or relate to others. In fact, I could hardly move or speak, and acting was an impossibility. To add insult to injury, the girls in my dormitory held a séance. I didn't participate, which left me ostracised, and the spiritual disturbance aroused unbearable torment in my head and body.

On a good note, this increased my desire to learn from Grandpa's book on communion. I followed its friendly pages from Friday to Sunday, and took it with me to 8 a.m. communion in the church my parents used to attend. Few people were there, but in those forty-five minutes I found peace and a sense of cleansing I'd never known before, although I knew I'd met something like it in the garden with Grandpa. That now seemed such a long time ago, when I'd been small and Grandpa was well and always there. Now he was seriously ill, alternating between hospital and convalescing.

The years from thirteen to fifteen were very hard, but during that time I discovered the God I'd never known personally to be real – and personal. I had continued to pray my prayer to have a pony by my birthday on 19th May 1966. The possibility grew when Grandpa gave me money as an inheritance. It wasn't a lot, but it could buy a horse. Seven days before the day in question my best friend phoned to say a local dealer had a three-year-old skewbald for sale. Her family had several horses and knew my passion. They let me ride occasionally but their horses were show jumpers so they had to be careful not to interrupt their training regime. The family offered all sorts of help if I took on the pony. My friend even offered to look for grazing for me, and found some within twenty-four hours. Somehow Dad was persuaded to go and see the pony. It was very green and threw me off when a plane flew overhead, although the dealer said I fell well! Dad was still keen and agreed to let me buy the pony with Grandpa's money. So, incredibly, on my birthday, the deal was done and I had a pony of my own.

I should explain that I wasn't normally even allowed a party on my birthday. As a special treat, I would be allowed one friend back for tea but she had to spend the evening in polite conversation with my parents. We couldn't play on our own – I guess, in case I said something. Not surprisingly, friends didn't like that so by this birthday it was just a day of school and homework. It wasn't until I was getting ready for bed that I realised what had happened. Alicia had confirmed the field for grazing. Dad had done the deal. Arrangements for the pony's arrival were all in place. He would arrive on 5th June, but he was mine from 19th May! My prayer had been answered. I remember it to this day; my face was full of soap and as I rinsed and reached for the towel, a voice in my head said, "Now do you believe I'm real?" It was so clear and penetrating I missed the towel. I was literally stopped in my tracks. I wanted to laugh and cry and shout all at the same time.

The pony arrived and we called him Jonty. He was adorable. Dad seemed to enjoy him and helped me a lot with his arrival, his care, and his fencing. Over and above all this, however, was the voice that said, "Now do you believe I'm real?" It threw me into a different quest. There was no more debate for me now. I'd met Grandpa's God in a powerful way. All I wanted was to pursue Him and know Him better. I continued to use my communion companion and never failed to attend the 8 a.m. service. Some of my torment seemed to ease for a while.

I now work with a church for youth who wouldn't normally attend church. Our passion is that they encounter the God they've never known, and live the difference. I hold that passion because it happened for me all those years ago. It was clearly God who did it. Living the difference wasn't quite so easy, but He has gradually broken into my life more and more. His relentless love has carried me and changed me to bring me to the place I'm in today. Now I can help others to break free from untold bondage. All I can do is bring them to Him to love them as He knows best.

It's been a long, hard journey, but He never fails us. From 19th May 1966 onwards, I knew God existed and I knew He knew me very personally. What a great foundation we have in Him – He really is an anchor in every storm. It's not about the pony and the date; it's about knowing Him and His loving presence. The story of the pony didn't end well, nor did other stories in my life, but through it all His love remains. Whatever the storm of opposition, with God there's always a way through further into His glory, His love manifest for me and in me.

12

A painful interlude

Weeks have passed since I've written, but God and His people are faithful so here I am, once more encouraged to keep going. This is a raw day. Writing about my life and struggles from the age of ten to fourteen became too much to handle even now. That's often a sign that something is rumbling deep within me, that some of my past experience has locked in another lie, or several lies. When this happens, I ask my faithful husband and my church leader to pray with me. Not all vicars are as pastorally trained and gifted, but God led Steve and me to this patient, faithful friend many years ago.

By God's grace we still work, worship, and minister together. I have had many helpers through secular counselling and in-depth prayer ministry who have taught me a great deal for which I am grateful. There are, however, dangers and pitfalls in any model because our only true healer is Jesus and what He's done for us on the cross.

Psalm 16 is one of my life psalms. It is so clear that God is my Lord and my chosen portion and that I have no good apart from Him. When a model of ministry, or a person, or even a secular model, begins to be exalted above Jesus as Lord, alarm bells begin to ring for me. The result or breakthrough can become the goal, and the method or person is seen as the way to that goal. We begin to seek the gift instead of the giver and Jesus ceases to be our chosen Lord and Saviour. As the Bible says, "Who has bewitched you?"[7]

The Christian walk is a battle. Romans 8 makes this clear and so does Psalm 16, but Jesus holds on to us and never leaves or forsakes us. We simply have to keep choosing Him.

What Steve and I have learned from our friend and helper in prayer is to keep pressing into God. This minister is adamant that God is there, that He was always there, and that He will always answer. No problem is too great or too hidden for Him. He has dealt with everything the enemy could ever throw at anybody, on the cross. He has conquered evil and risen from the dead, and lives in us and with us for eternity if we have turned from our sinful, selfish ways and invited him to be Lord of our lives.

If God appears not to be answering me in prayer, or seems to be distant, I know the block is with me. All I have to do is ask Him what's in the way and what to do about it. Sometimes, like yesterday, I need friends to help me through. Steve and my pastor are faithful and confident to do that. Many of the lies that trap me have been sealed in through trauma and abuse inflicted on me when I was young. In prayer, I often need to touch the memories of that trauma and find Jesus' truth and presence. The fear and emotion can be intense when a fearful memory is revisited and I need support, guidance, and encouragement to keep turning to God for His help and His wisdom. That's what this faithful friend and Steve do for me in times of ministry. Jesus needed friends to pray with Him in Gethsemane. In His humanity, the prospect of the biggest battle with Satan was overwhelming, but He found the courage to fight through for us. Now we can enjoy the fruits of His suffering as we bring our suffering to Him. Satanism turns the truth of God and Christianity on its head. In times of ministry it is this truth and the power of Jesus' death and resurrection that set me free. It is not a power encounter; Jesus has already won. It's a truth encounter. I need to put lies to death, shake off Satan's hold, and embrace the power of Jesus' wonderful resurrection from the dead.

---

[7] Galatians 3:1 (NIV)

Any drama, manifestation, and emotion encountered in these times of prayer can be intimidating but simply turning to Him is always the path to peace and release. The memories I encountered yesterday were from experiences I had as a three-year-old child. They were extremely painful and traumatic. It will take time for me to grieve that this really happened in and through my family, but God comforts those who mourn. His comfort never fails. I can then comfort others with the comfort I've received from God.[8]

I don't feel I need to go into the sad detail of the memories I revisited yesterday. What I do want to do is honour my pastor, my husband, and Jesus for their love and faithfulness, and celebrate yet another miracle of healing. It is so simple and so profound. At the end of the day, the thrust of ministry is to help hurting people to seek and find God, and choose His way through their valley of shadows[9].

The prayer time on Monday ended abruptly. It seems the trauma got too much for me, so God gently said, "Enough now." I spent all week talking and listening to God about that prayer time and have realised that the intense trauma wasn't so much in the event we prayed about as an event that followed, and my fear from that subsequent memory. I will take time to see if I can meet God for myself in the untouched memories. If I can't, I'll ask for help again, but it's worth taking time alone first.

One thing we seek to do for our clients is equip them to press into God by themselves as well as to know when to ask for help. There is a healthy dependence in facilitating emotional healing. Hurting people often find unhelpful ways of coping alone. These are based on lies about God, life, and relationships, and can bear unhealthy fruits such as manipulation, repression, and isolation. Counsellors, pastoral workers, and prayer ministers need to be able to recognise co-dependent behaviour and model, teach, and practise healthy independence, dependence, and inter-dependence. In churches, this is crucial learning for pastoral leaders, teams, and prayer ministers. As part of our teaching,

---

[8] See 2 Corinthians 1
[9] See Psalm 23

Steve and I work with church ministers who then often send their pastoral teams to us for training. We then have a more consultant and specialist role, helping people who are stuck in that walk. Our Bespoke strapline is, "We help you follow where you see Jesus leading." We may need to help someone know how to see where Jesus is leading, but that's exactly what must happen. If we are His sheep – and as Jesus says in John 10:3-6 His sheep "listen to" and "know" His voice – then we can all hear Him. No one needs to be overly dependent on us or on others. Romans 12:5 explores this healthy dependence and inter-dependence.

This is another reason Steve and I love to work with church leaders: to help them build their local body. We believe that the local church is key to God's design for the Body of Christ. Ephesians 4 and Romans 12 speak beautifully about how the local church body needs to love and build itself up into Jesus. This is spiritual maturity. We are keen that our ministry, Bespoke, should never become a para-church organisation. Instead, our heart is to serve churches and to help their leaders in any way we can. In Steve's words, we also love to help the "broken-hearted become brave-hearted".

Sometimes people ask us to teach and train others in the "Bespoke model", but we chose the name Bespoke precisely because we don't have a model. In the scriptures, we see Jesus working differently with each individual. He loves each one and turns him or her to His Father, helping and healing through God's power in wonderful ways, and we see this in our work. We have learned and experienced both good and bad from many models and methods of prayer and counselling. Prophetic people have said to us, "Your tool-bags are full. The journey you have travelled with God has been your training ground. Now that you've learned to seek Him, find Him, and follow Him, go and help others do the same. Be Jesus to others and sing His love to them in many different ways. His love is like music. You play it to people on different instruments according to their character and needs." So I don't think we'll ever become a huge organisation. In the words of Romans 12, this is simply our way of using His gifts to us to serve the beautiful, cherished body of His Son Jesus Christ. To Him be all the glory and all the honour.

He is so worthy that to sing His praises anywhere near loud and long enough I would need the help of angels. The older I become, the greater my awe is at the wonder of Jesus' death on the cross and the meaning of His resurrection and life in us. It will take heaven and eternity to understand all that, but I'm loving living in the mystery, and seeing the fruit of the travail of His soul in the lives of all He graciously brings to us for help and prayer.

13

Jonty enjoyed

Let's return to poor Jonty and what transpired after God gave me my miracle pony.

I love the way God is partnering with me in writing this book. I really couldn't have done it without Him. It might sound like a cliché, but it's also the absolute truth. Each day that I've written, I've come to God and said, "Please show me what to write today." I'm sure that, at times, some of my own thinking has come through, but overall I know His will has been promoted in what's come out on the paper in front of me. I feel honoured, humbled, and excited. Sometimes I've read these words back to myself and been truly blessed and uplifted. I've been keen that this writing should never be out of bitterness or self-pity; instead I want to glorify Him and encourage others.

Yesterday we prayed with a dear friend who ministers to men and women who have suffered the havoc wreaked by war, tsunami, and sex trafficking. Their devastation is beyond my imagining: some have lost six or seven relatives in one go; others have been treated like animals, lined up for men to use for money that goes largely to their "owners" and in small part to their starving families.

This is evil and injustice at its worst. My past was hard, but if my healing can point others to Jesus and His love, compassion, and wisdom – to how He holds the keys to eternal life – then this book is worth all the effort and pain it's taken to write.

I just spent a wonderful hour with Jesus, experiencing His gentle ministry to my pain over the loss of Jonty. I've been there before with Him, but each time my healing has gone deeper. Some traumas need gradual healing. God never takes you "beyond what you can bear"[10]. "For he knows our frame; he remembers that we are dust."[11]

So what did happen to Jonty? The answer is that I'm not really sure. I only know my story from my perspective and the light God gives me on it.

Jonty was a lovely pony, but he was also very young. With hindsight, a first pony should probably be older. However, my lovely friend's family promised to help me with him and were confident we could mould him into something special. He had a kind eye and a willingness to learn, and he liked me a lot; we bonded from our first day together. Although I was quite scared when I had to manage him alone, every time I found myself in this position I prayed for God's help and wisdom. I was confident He had given me this pony, and He never failed me.

One day Jonty opened his own gate and went for a wander on the busy roads around his field. Fortunately, Dad was good with animals, having grown up around farms with carthorses and riding and tending animals much bigger than himself from a young age. When Jonty ran out on to the road, Dad helped me to find him and lead him back home to safety without a head collar, which we'd forgotten to take in our panic.

That day was a bonding experience for Dad and me, and from then on we began to care for Jonty together. Dad put up fencing, called on Jonty on his way home from work and loved to chat about his antics. We developed a way of "riding out" together. I'd mount Jonty and Dad would lead him over the intimidating railway bridge to Rushford racecourse. Dad would go back and collect the car while I walked Jonty on the grass at the edge of the course. It was called the "straight mile", and it was certainly very straight. Unfortunately, all it said to Jonty was

---

[10] 1 Corinthians 10:13 (NIV)
[11] Psalm 103:14 (ESV)

"gallop". I could generally hold him back, but once Dad's car passed us (he'd drive to the other end of the mile to meet me) Jonty would be desperate to catch up and we'd fly like the wind down that straight mile. Dad loved his connection with Jonty. I was terrified every time, but I loved the growing bond with my dad. We had found a language and a pleasure that we could share; this was all I'd ever wanted.

My mum was alarmed about our Jonty stories, and my friend's family also expressed concern. A young pony needed schooling. Freedom to gallop as he did wasn't healthy, and Jonty began to take control from me, especially when I rode without Dad. For some reason, Dad seemed to resent advice from anyone, including my friend's family. He believed he knew exactly how to manage my pony and that was all that mattered to him. I began to feel rather pushed out; but the bond with Dad meant even more to me than my relationship with my precious pony.

14

Jonty spoilt

The grass in Jonty's field had some very overgrown patches. I was leading him through there one day, with Dad cheering me on. He loved tutoring me. I was nervous in the long grass and Jonty was a strong pony, but if Dad said it, I was going to do it. I would do anything to please him and I had been highly trained in repressing my own wisdom, judgement, and insights. A cat was sleeping in the long grass and, startled by our approach, it jumped up underneath Jonty and ran between his front legs. Jonty reared several times and I fell. Somehow, I landed under Jonty and as he jumped off his powerful hind legs to bolt away, he placed his back hoof just above my groin and I took the full weight.

> *Surgeons, when I was thirty-five, were perplexed to find my appendix and bowel imprinted with a clear horseshoe shape. For me, it explained some of the medical problems I'd suffered until that time. Once my appendix was removed and other damaged tissue repaired, my health improved significantly.*

When I was fourteen, and in their care, my parents were reluctant to seek medical help. I fainted several times immediately after the accident, but Dad shouted me to my feet and insisted I catch my pony and walk with him. This is good training as a general principle. In this case, however, I think I was too badly injured. I was nauseous and blacking out, but I was trained to tap into ritual ways of pushing through pain. "It's mind over matter," was Dad's mantra.

Eventually I led Jonty around the field and we were able to untack, settle, and leave him munching grass. On the way home Dad warned me not to talk about the accident. He was clear that if I said too much someone would take Jonty away. I was told to be extremely careful in what I said to Mum, or she would also want to be rid of Jonty. So I walked into the house as boldly as I could and tried to make light of the incident. Pain was getting the better of me, however, so I went to lie on my bed after struggling through lunch.

The pain grew worse and a large red lump grew in my groin area. It was bigger than a horse's hoof and was raised nearly two inches high. I was very scared. Dad refused to visit me while I was in bed, and seemed to be instructing Mum. She refused to look at what I now know was a large haematoma (or soft tissue bleed). If the surface skin had broken I would have bled profusely, but I prayed that wouldn't happen. I was frightened of the extent of my injury, of saying too much and losing Jonty, and of upsetting my newfound relationship with Dad. Mum said he wasn't cross, but I was troubled that he didn't want to see me. She said he was busy with his job and with worrying about Jonty's care. She also told me that he was not happy with my being in bed and off school. After a week in bed I persuaded Mum to phone the GP, but she was reluctant, saying that Dad felt it was all in my mind. To be fair, the haematoma had shrunk a little and looked darker but I was worried about what might have happened underneath the wound. Dad told Mum I needed to learn to handle my anxiety. I think Mum was genuinely concerned and felt torn between her concerns over my condition and Dad's instruction. She visited me often, bringing food, but daren't stay with me long.

I finally persuaded her to phone the doctor one day when Dad was at work. I told her my school would want to know what had happened and what the doctor had said. Whether she phoned or not, I'll never know, but she told me that she had. According to Mum, the doctor had said, "Don't worry. She'll be fine. Just lie in bed until the swelling and bruising goes down." I wasn't sure it was merely swelling and bruising, but after two more weeks in bed the haematoma had subsided and become a horseshoe-shaped bruise. I began to be able to walk to the toilet in my third week after the accident, rather than crawl on all fours.

I was sent to school as soon as I could move. Exercising mind control as best I could, I managed my lessons without complaining. I made light of the accident and prayed that I'd be back to normal as soon as possible. I was terrified of losing Jonty or dishonouring Mum and Dad. Several people asked if I'd been to hospital or seen a doctor. I put a stop to these conversations and questions by telling them what Mum had reported and by moving as freely as I could, however painful.

After six weeks, I began to feel more like my old self. Eight weeks later, my friend Alicia's mum, Frieda, was giving me a lesson on Jonty. I was struggling to use my right leg to direct him in a circle. Frieda was kind, and came over to ask exactly what had happened in the accident. For some reason, I trusted her and told her the truth. I thought Dad wouldn't mind because she loved Jonty and me and wanted to help us in any way she could, but I couldn't have been more mistaken. When she heard about the details of the accident she was very concerned and asked if I'd been to hospital and had X-rays, assuming that would naturally happen. When she realised it hadn't she became perplexed and angry with my parents, accusing them of gross neglect. I knew immediately that I'd said too much. She talked with her husband and they offered to help me with Jonty over the summer. They said that owning a pony was a big responsibility – something people often didn't realise until they had one; there was no shame in not knowing and they believed I could get on well with Jonty; they applauded my potential and his, and our growing bond with each other.

I was excited; my accident seemed to be working for good. I'd read about this in Romans in my Bible[12] and gleefully told Dad all Frieda had said. But his reaction surprised me – he seemed jealous of the attention and affirmation Alicia's family were giving me, and became furious at Frieda's suggestion that I have an X-ray. He forbade me to have any contact with her ever again, or to allow her or her family near Jonty. He was adamant that he knew everything about horses and that it was my selfish childishness and inadequacy that had caused all my problems.

I was sad and embarrassed, but had to tell Alicia what Dad had said. It was little surprise then that when Dad wanted me to go to the north for the summer vacation, Alicia's parents refused to let her look after Jonty for me. At first, I'd assumed we'd take Jonty with us. Grandpa would be there, and there was grazing and stabling and miles of wonderful countryside. Dad simply refused to discuss the matter, and instead left Jonty in the care of a child who had no experience of

---

[12] See Romans 8:28

owning a pony, no parental help, and little riding ability. I was forbidden to make any complaint.

We spent that summer at Grandpa's, but he was unwell and didn't protest about Jonty's absence. He had no energy for conflict and I saw little of him. That holiday was hard and it only grew harder. I was angry to be separated from Jonty. We had no horse trailer but hiring one shouldn't have been difficult. Maybe the problem was finances – I'll never know, but I do know I was frustrated and helpless. My money from Grandpa and other hard-earned finances had already been spent on Jonty and his tack and fencing, and winter feeding was going to be a problem. I was losing confidence that Dad would come to the rescue. He seemed stressed, and I didn't dare broach the subject of any of my anxieties.

I was also worried about Jonty's carer for the summer, Emelia. She was at grammar school with me, but not as academic as I was and I think that caused her resentment. Her father had died suddenly of a heart attack a few years earlier, and she was emotionally troubled. Dad wanted her to have Jonty for the summer because he felt she was needy and he wanted to help her. I felt selfish for wanting my pony for myself, and worse for doubting Emelia's ability to handle him, but he was only three years old and very green. It wasn't pride on my part, which is what Dad led me to believe. I would have loved Alicia's family's experienced help. I struggled with strong emotions of anger, grief, and anxiety. To add insult to injury, Grandpa was in hospital or convalescence most of the holiday which left me free for night-time rituals. I was older now, so these felt even worse. I was also seriously seeking God, which seemed to hamper my ritual training and ability. The punishment is severe for those who betray the circle, and the hardest thing was seeing Dad dishonoured and punished for my failure.

> *I'm not going into a lot of detail about these rituals. Steve and my vicar have prayed with me through horrendous memories from these times. I see no benefit in sharing in detail the depravity I witnessed and experienced. It's taken me a long time to get my head around how a parent can take a child into such situations. I've concluded that there is a point where evil takes over and has such a hold that human reason and compassion no longer exist. There's a switch that occurs which*

can be seen clearly in a person's eyes. I could spot this in daylight but at night it was harder.

Those ritual nights were full of darkness, flashes of lights, fire, and confusion.

I'm going to leave it there for now. I don't want to remember too much. It has complicated my grief since Dad has died. The mixture of anger, pain, confusion, and longing are hard to carry, and exhausting.

My fears about Emelia were well-founded. Barely one week into the holiday we received a phone call. Grandpa didn't have a telephone so a call was a serious matter, and someone at the pub or the village shop passed on the message. Dad then had a phone conversation with someone in Rushford, although I'm not quite sure who. Emelia had apparently tied Jonty to a fixed rail. I suspect she hadn't used breakable bailing twine for the connecting loop which normally acts as a safety mechanism should the pony seek to break free. Something happened as she went to saddle him and he bolted, unearthing the post and rails. He ended up pinned upside down on the ground, unharmed (so I was told, but after being released he became impossible to catch so I don't know how anyone could know he wasn't injured).

Emelia had ridden Jonty before this incident, but he had apparently discovered how to throw her off by galloping under trees in the field so she couldn't stay aboard him. Even before the fence trauma occurred she had been losing confidence. After it she refused to visit him at all. Poor Jonty was now considered wild and dangerous.

My assumption was that we would go home and fetch Jonty to comfort and reassure him. The lovely family who owned Rush and Reggie were keen to meet him and were more than capable of helping others to resettle him. Now, maybe, we could bring him to the north to be with us after all! To my horror, Dad refused to return to Rushford. Confident that he could sort him out, his conclusion was to leave Jonty unattended until we returned home. In the course of conversations to which I was not allowed to contribute, mention was made that Jonty may need to be shot. I couldn't shake the thought, and neither could I trust God that this fate wouldn't befall my beloved pony. I felt so alone and confused. God had provided Jonty but evil seemed to be getting the upper hand. The only way I could cope that summer was to re-enter evil practices and to carry on my past training.

Mum caught me performing ritual behaviour one day that summer. She was angry and upset. I'm not sure she knew much about the experiences I had been taken through from babyhood. To quell her anger, I tried to explain my fears that Jonty might be shot. She told me not to be ridiculous, but added that we should never have got him in the first place. I felt bereft. God seemed distant, Grandpa was in hospital, and I was trapped.

> *A child is dependent and helpless. Parents have authority, and a child depends on them for everything, even food and clothing. Safety is another essential that a child needs.*

My only way to feel safe was to do whatever my parents wanted in those lonely days. Even so, I failed. The family hated my being low and anxious. I was tired and made to feel a failure in the rituals. Grandpa was likely to die; God was nowhere to be found; I daren't even seek Him. I was filled with rage but also fear. I tried self-harming to focus my pain and confused emotion. I had to make sure it didn't show because they'd know in the rituals if I damaged my body rather than using their training. I was beginning to fall apart.

Mum had taught me self-hypnosis, which her GP had recommended for her own troubles. It helped me into a trance-like state at night and fantasy through the day. In the longer term, the hypnosis led to horrendous nightmares and daytime terrors. But God wasn't totally out of the picture. Although I was only rarely allowed to visit Grandpa, when I did I became aware of God, and was impacted by Grandpa's love and stability. He spoke of God and clung to Him, and carried a peace and joy I couldn't ignore. Eventually, I asked for God's help. My prayer was simply, "Please do something!" – and He did.

A song came to mind that we'd been taught at junior school in my happy days with Mrs Knightley and the headmaster Mr Duggan and his wife. I did so well in those last years of junior school that I'd been presented with a Bible as a character prize. It meant the world to me but I found that whenever I tried to read it, I would shake, my vision would become blurred, and I would develop a headache. During that holiday, I tried very hard to read it to find some comfort but these negative side-effects grew too much. This song, however, brought me a peace that lasted to the end of that dismal summer:

When at night I go to sleep
Fourteen angels watch.
Two my head are guarding
Two my feet are guiding
Two are on my right hand
Two are on my left hand
Two who warmly cover
Two who o'er me hover
Two to whom 'tis given
To guide my steps to heaven.

From Hansel & Gretel, composed by Engelbert Humperdink and premiered in Weimar 23/12/1893

This song helped me turn my thoughts to God. He has since shown me that He was helping me come close to Him in a very personal way. The song covered my whole body; I needed to know each part of me was safe and acceptable to someone.

In ministry, I love the way God comes close to people in ways that are truly personal to them. That's what He did for me. I've no idea how. I don't have expert theological knowledge about angels, but I know that something and someone carried me through a summer of anguish. Throughout my life, whatever the nightmare, God has come through and carried me. In the valley of the shadow He has sought me, found me, and been with me. Steve and I love to help people find Him in their valley of the shadow. Even where the enemy appears to have the upper hand, God breaks through clearly – and far more powerfully – holding the victory Jesus won for us on the cross.

Let's end this summer holiday in praise. Pause for a moment and thank Him for the cross and resurrection power He's won for us. He never fails. Hold on to that as you read the rest of my story. It got worse, far worse, before it got better, but all the way God walked with me. That's why Jesus died and rose again, so we could know Him for eternity and never need to be alone. It's a mystery, but it's more real than anything else I've ever known, or will ever know.

Writing a book is hard work! It's probably because I'm writing my very personal, painful story. I write in ink and Steve converts what I say to text by reading it using a speech recognition tool called "Dragon". (This can have some ridiculous results.) I normally read through the script before I let faithful friends and family vet the latest instalment of my writing. I came to write today after a week off with more infections, and when I discovered that the last ten pages had been sent out without being edited, I lost heart and moved into deep anxiety, shame, and hopelessness. Steve's response, and no doubt that of my other readers, was, "That's really not a big deal. People won't mind." But for me, old anxieties about being seen as a fool, not being understood, and fear of serious reprisal have almost prevented me from writing any more.

This level of struggle is significant. Nowadays, I can recognise what's going on and deal with it. I repent of returning to old, untrue ways of thinking which raise old, unhealthy, inaccurate feelings. I forgive those who cause me to believe these things and forgive myself for still believing them. Satan has been a liar from the beginning and is the father of lies (John 8). Instead, I receive Jesus' forgiveness and am then in a position to rebuke anything that's got hold of me through my believing these lies. Today I have rebuked shame, fear of rejection, and mockery. I tell anything of the enemy to leave me now and go under Jesus' feet. That seems the best place for anything of the enemy to be (whatever really happens in the spiritual world, Jesus knows and that's good enough for me). Then I ask Jesus to replace all that is unhealthy with His truth and blessing so I can walk on in the freedom of what He gives. Today He gave me encouragement, acceptance, a thankful heart, and trust in my friends. Now I feel able to pick up writing again.

This way of praying is a useful Scripture-based tool which we teach our clients and others who ask us to pray with them. It's based on Jesus' teaching through the scriptures about the enemy, repentance, forgiveness, and the authority given to all disciples by Jesus[13] to rebuke the enemy and send him away. It frees us to receive God's truth and comfort again, and to walk on in the strength of that.

As you can see, it's a tool I use often. The Christian walk is a daily battle, but Jesus has already won the victory on the cross

---

[13] See Matthew 28:18-20

and in the resurrection. This way of praying helps us to appropriate all He has done for us, in our walk with Him. My belief is that being a Christian isn't just a one-time decision; it's a continuing walk, an ongoing commitment to living a new life in His strength.[14]

---

[14] See Galatians 2:20

15

Jonty lost

So what *did* happen to Jonty? When we came home from the north we found him in a very bad state. Horses are herd animals and prey animals, not predators, and they need company. A pony that lives alone experiences fear. No one told us that back in Jonty's day. I have since learned that a horse left alone in a field can feel as if it's going to die.

Jonty couldn't be caught, so his coat was unkempt and his hooves were overgrowing his shoes. One day I tried to catch him quietly on my own, hoping that the memory of our bond would return to him. When I was unsuccessful I tried praying, but that didn't work either. I got very close to Jonty at one point, and then a fearful memory from my accident of his strength and weight caused me to back off. Suddenly, a rage like I'd experienced with Reggie rose in me again, and something in me snapped. I lost control and screamed and shouted and hit a tree with his head collar. Jonty fled in fear and I knew our relationship was broken. I felt stupid and alone, angry with myself and confused. Now I believed God would remove Himself from me as well. I wanted to cry but felt I didn't deserve that luxury. When I allowed a few tears, rage and fear began to rise again. I withdrew into a dark and dangerous place within myself, which took me deeper into using my ritual training, and further into fear and withdrawal.

Dad managed to catch Jonty a couple of times. The horse dealer who sold him to us gave us a collar to leave on him permanently and suggested we give Jonty back to him until the springtime. He hoped that a winter running free with other ponies would ease his sad memories and render him ready to be broken in again and re-schooled. At this kind suggestion, I felt God was caring for me after all.

I loved the thought of Jonty running free with friends. I'd asked God's forgiveness for losing my temper and I felt He had heard my prayer. Sadly, this dream winter never materialised.

Maybe Dad was worried that Jonty had reared up when he had finally managed to get hold of him. I argued that the winter's rest and re-schooling could solve that. Dad agreed, or so he led me to believe. Plans were made for Jonty's removal, and I felt happier.

Then, one morning in October, I was getting ready for school and Dad was outside cleaning a head collar. Jack, the horse dealer, had sent the head collar for Jonty so he could take him to his winter grazing. I was stunned when, with his back to me, Dad said, "I've sold your pony." I wanted to question, protest, argue, scream – but Dad followed with a firm, "I want no questions and nothing said about it. It's done and final."

I don't know how I managed school that day. The following evening, I went to see Jonty, to pray, apologise, and say goodbye. When I got there, his field was empty. The gate was wide open. The field owner said a man had taken my pony.

I went home expecting anger because I was late, but I felt sure Mum and Dad would understand my actions. When I arrived home, I was met with blind fury from Dad. He had found the empty field and was somehow convinced I'd taken Jonty and hidden him. Nothing I said would convince Dad otherwise. He tried to batter the truth out of me, but I was as baffled as he was.

I begged him to phone Jack and either eventually he did or Jack phoned him. I was beyond knowing what was going on.

Later that evening, I was alone in my bedroom; tea had been out of the question. Dad came and told me how kind Jack was, as if none of the earlier evening trauma had happened. He'd discovered that Jack had felt it was too hard for me to box Jonty and had decided to fetch my pony while I was at school to save me the pain of saying goodbye. Dad thought I should be grateful for Jack's kindness. He also told me that Jonty had been no problem to catch, so, in his words, all was well.

For me, all was certainly *not* well.

I had no idea how to handle myself or my pain at this series of outrageous injustices.

16

Aftermath

I've put off writing for almost two weeks. Part of me wanted simply to get it done, so the weight and the pain of the memories would lift. But when I've come to write, the weight has increased. I've found myself feeling unable to face going back to my fifteenth and sixteenth years. Writing about the day I lost Jonty has left me quite depressed. "Sad" may be a better word, but it's not sufficiently strong. It's an agony of soul that lies deep inside me. During these days, I have been blessed to read Mark 14 in my beloved Amplified Bible. Verse 33 says Jesus was "deeply troubled and depressed"[15] in Gethsemane. I was encouraged by this. Depression is often debated in Christian circles. Some say it's due to lies we believe, or lack of faith. When I read Mark 14, I sensed God pointing out verse 33. He reminded me of the time my lovely GP helped me through the loss of our first child. Many people said I was depressed and several tried to encourage me to trust God and have more faith. I went to talk with my doctor because I was confused and concerned. His comment reassured and released me. He said, "You're not depressed, Helen, you're grieving and that's a healthy process!"

Depression is part of the grieving process. Jesus knows what it's like. He doesn't condemn or challenge. There may be lies in

---

[15] Mark 14:33 (AMPC)

our sad places where hope is gone, but there are reasons for these lies having a hold in our hearts.

The word and memories God gave me from Mark 14 have helped me return to writing. The encouragement of friends and family who have read what I've written so far has also given me faith to carry on writing. Thank you, God, for my GP, my friends, and my family.

So here we go again!

Jonty was taken on a Friday. I don't remember the subsequent days. Most vividly etched in my mind is the Sunday night after that Friday. I went to bed with all sorts of feelings that I couldn't process. Just as Dad had ordered, I said nothing else about Jonty and asked no questions. There was no point. When Dad said no he always meant *no*. I've a feeling I said very little that weekend, because there was nothing to say. My mind and heart were full of grief about Jonty. I'm sure I was angry too, which frightened me. I didn't want my anger or rage to seep out at home; I would be too vulnerable.

By Sunday night sleep was out of the question. I felt like I was bursting. Alone in my room, lying in bed, my tears began to flow uncontrollably. I tried to roll over and keep quiet, but my sobbing was getting louder. I sensed a voice – maybe God's, I don't know – saying, "It's all right to cry. Someone needs to know how you feel." With this encouragement, I let the sobbing continue. There was a beautiful moment when Mum came into my bedroom and sat on my bed. She seemed to truly care for me and I grew braver when she put an arm around my shoulders. In my newfound courage, I told her how I felt that God had given me Jonty and how confused I felt that He'd now let me down. She brushed off any sense of God having given me Jonty, saying, "I don't know about that... but what I *do* know is God may seem to let us down, but really we know He never does." I was touched and taken aback by her willingness to mention God's name and her expression of faith in His goodness.

I hold on to that moment.

Things changed for the worse after that. Dad came into my room and sat on the opposite side of the bed. He asked what the noise was and Mum explained that I was upset about Jonty. I was scared he'd be angry, but he wasn't; it was far worse than that. For a while the three of us sat together, and I felt strangely blessed and comforted, thinking that

God had brought good out of Jonty's downfall. Then I realised Dad was sobbing. His crying grew louder and he began to wail. Mum and I turned towards him and he looked at me and said, "You've broken my heart!" I'm still not sure what he meant, or how I could have broken his heart. I thought I was the one who was upset because he had sold my pony. I concluded that my expression of grief had hurt him, but I didn't know what to do with that.

I soon learned, however, never to express my feelings again. As Dad continued to sob and say, "You've broken my heart, broken my heart, broken my heart..." Mum's demeanour changed. She removed her arm from my shoulder, pushed me, stood up, and shouted, "Now look what you've done! You'll be the death of him! You'll destroy your father with your selfishness! How could you do this?" She moved to comfort him and they left my room together.

I was suddenly alone. God had confused me again. I thought He'd said I needed to let out my grief but now I'd caused disaster and even the risk of death to my father. I was scared, but I had a sense that what I'd done wasn't wrong. I could even feel God's presence. In my confusion and fear, I moved into a place of utter silence. For four days I was mute, trapped inside myself. I couldn't speak to anyone. I was afraid if I uttered a single word I might cry again.

On the Thursday of that week a gentle girl called Tracey took me to one side in the gym corridor. Something in her caring manner and small stature gave me courage not to run from her. She took hold of my wrist and said, "Helen, something is very wrong. Can you tell me about it?" I managed to stutter, "Dad's sold my pony." She was aghast. She had so many questions but I couldn't say any more. I was shaking, trying to hold back the tears. I didn't dare say more for fear of hurting my father. Tracey's concern helped me, but it also frightened me.

> *Before we go any further I want to strike a balance in my writing. I can look at my past, and particularly this Jonty experience, and be angry and judgemental. I haven't told this story often, but when I have, loving friends and ministers have reacted with indignation against my parents. Anger at their behaviour is appropriate. Acknowledging the injustice and wrongly-placed blame is also healthy. I have needed help to acknowledge my anger and the wrong done to me. My silence, independence, and confusion over the years that followed were*

part of the cause of my subsequent depressions at the ages of twenty-two and twenty-five.

17

No more visits to the village

Grandpa was in hospital more and more often after Jonty left. He had severe heart problems which required long spells in hospitals and convalescent homes. It was hard to find help for Grandpa when he lived at home. Sadly, the couple in his bungalow didn't offer the care he'd hoped for, but he hadn't the heart to evict them.

In time, Grandpa decided to sell his beautiful house. I think he realised that the rituals had not ended for me. When he was ill and away from home, I was easily accessible and we visited the north often, on the pretext of seeing him.

Grandpa offered my dad a choice: to let him live with us so we could have the money from his estate, or to use the money to pay for him to go into a home. Dad's preference would have been to keep Grandpa's house and bungalow, but that wasn't an option. Grandpa was determined to sell so that both Dad and I could be free from the rituals. As Annabella had gone to college, it was now feasible for him to live with us.

So the estate was sold, and Grandpa moved to Rushford. I was delighted. I'm sure that's how I survived my years from fifteen to seventeen. It was hard at times, however – especially at first. Grandpa was very ill, and when the blood couldn't circulate to his brain he lost all sense of where he was. It's distressing when someone you love fails to recognise you and is clearly living in another time. He often went back to the death of his son at the age of nineteen, during the war. Watching Grandpa's grief was heart-breaking.

Dad became depressed when Grandpa's house was sold. Mum was physically ill, and Annabella was unhappy at college. These were hard days to begin to study for my O Level exams. To add insult to injury, I kept failing my mocks, however hard I studied.

I also was trying to recover from several appalling rituals. When I was fifteen I made a significant decision. I don't consciously recall it, but I do remember a horrendous ritual where my father and I were punished for my faith in God and my inability to renounce Him. I say "inability" advisedly, because all I remember is being unable to do what my ritual training required and unable to renounce Him despite the anger that aroused in my persecutors. My expulsion involved some experiences I won't describe in detail. It is enough to say they included extreme sexual, physical, and emotional abuse.

> *I don't feel this was an act of heroism in any way. Left to myself I think I'd have done what they wanted. I'm not really sure. In recent years, I've had help to talk to God about the anger I felt that He enabled me to make such a big step of faith at that time. The trauma of the repercussions from that has gradually surfaced and left me vulnerable to periods of doubt and enemy attack and intimidation in my current life and ministry which I have had to find help to address.*
>
> *I couldn't face the horror of what happened to me until I was well into my fifties. I still have other memories to deal with now. These horrors lock in lies that creep up and torment me in my current life. I thank God for my husband, friends, ministers, and children, who help me through these times. Now these rough times are few and far between but I endeavour to stay open to having help and ministry, should that seem necessary or helpful.*

Mum had serious back problems. As a very young child she'd been forced to carry coal up from the cellars in the children's home. While this had caused physical damage, the doctors were clear that much of her pain was psychological. She had suffered abuse of every kind: cruelty, gross neglect, and abandonment. She had never had any help to work through this as the war-time mentality focused more on advice to "grin and bear it" or "be strong and keep going". Counselling, in fact, developed out of the support given to soldiers to recover from World War II.

Mum was put on traction at home. She needed a bed with an end on it, and so needed to use mine. Grandpa had Annabella's room, so I took Mum's place in Dad's bedroom. They had twin beds by now, but it was still a recipe for disaster. I won't go into detail, but it's not hard to imagine what happened.

At this time Dad had decided to coach me in athletics. The school had recognised my sporting prowess and I was entered in city, regional, and county high-jump competitions. He had been an army athletics champion and, sadly, his training methods were brutal. Coupled with his sense of possessing me and my life and body, his keeping of boundaries was poor. When I damaged my knee tendons he insisted on "treating" me in the bath, and required full access into my bathroom. With my ritual training and personal confusion, I overrode my own feelings and kept silent about what seemed deeply wrong to me. I was left feeling sullied and unclean.

Dad pushed me to use my ritual mind control abilities to overcome my knee pain. Later he tried to use it to increase my performance in as many athletic sports as possible, but I wasn't a very good student. I was increasingly unhappy and confused, and failed in big competitions. Dad grew angrier and angrier and lost heart completely by the time I was sixteen. I knew I was a disappointment but I didn't know what to do about it.

At this point Grandpa's health improved. He realised life was not right at home and insisted on a bed downstairs in the dining room, so I could sleep in Annabella's room when Mum needed my bed. There was a good lock on Annabella's door; my sanity began to return.

Under the strain of ritual torment and confusion, I had begun to fail in school, but as I look back I see a beautiful thread of God's care and provision running through my life. When I was sixteen, two new teachers arrived at our school, one who taught religious education and the other physics. One of my friends shared the gospel with me one day after the physics teacher had talked to her class about sin and salvation. Amanda had been personally challenged and put the challenge to me. I was deeply troubled by my own sense of sin. This helped me choose to study religious education as an extra O Level during my lower sixth year. We had a lovely teacher called Mrs White who was also a Christian. As we studied the book of Mark, she wove in the gospel and brought Jesus to life. I loved those lessons. She had visited the Holy Land and brought us photographs of all the places in the Bible which we were studying. We studied Mark's Gospel for our exam. I was so excited by it and tried to learn all sixteen chapters off by heart. This really helped quieten the ritual chants, threats, and accusations that tormented my mind, day and night. God's Word has power to bring relief even from the darkest secret horrors. Our lives can be transformed by Jesus if we let Him in when He tries to get our attention. Maybe that's why I love the story of the Apostle Paul so much. God was trying to get my attention at this time, as Grandpa came to live with us in Rushford and loved to talk about the gospel.

Mrs White moved beyond the end of Mark to Acts. She used Paul's transformation from Saul to teach us all how our lives can be transformed and I was keen to know how Jesus could help me through life when Grandpa was "taken home". All these things, I believe, were God's provision in a dark, crucial time in my life. Mrs White and Grandpa helped bring me to a serious commitment to Christ when I was seventeen, but God had been very present in all the years before.

18

Downs and ups

After I lost Jonty I seemed unable to succeed in my exams. I worked hard, but my results dropped from A1 grades to well below failure. No one thought to query this and I was simply put into bottom sets in my worst subjects. The good news was that Tracey was also in those sets, and another girl called Barbara. These two had no axes to grind and nothing to prove in life. Many girls in their teenage years strive for success and popularity or sporting prowess, but Tracey and Barbara were content. They had discovered other values in life.

Tracey attended a speech and drama class outside school to which she invited me along. We went together for several years. There was an annual festival of speech and drama, with the whole class entering classes of their choice. I entered verse speaking, mime, drama (monologue), drama (Shakespeare), drama (duologue with Tracey), and storytelling. Other local festivals included Bible reading. This attracted me after my good experiences in junior school. So Tracey and I travelled to other festivals, especially those with a Bible reading competition. I loved Scripture and I also enjoyed reading aloud.

I began to win trophies. My confidence grew as my parents took a new interest in me. Tracey never won anything – she just enjoyed being there with me.

At school and church people began to pick up on my abilities. I think my mother asked the vicar if I could read a lesson in church, and he agreed. Mum or Dad may have done the same thing for me at school.

When I look back, I realise I chose melancholy pieces of drama and poetry, often about mourning and death. I had found a way of expressing some of the grief I carried about Jonty and my other losses. I was troubled, in later years, that I found light-hearted drama more difficult. I didn't always win with those pieces, so I avoided them. I did do well in storytelling, however. We were given three objects and had to weave an entertaining story around them. I loved the sense of "holding an audience". It wasn't always healthy for me – at times winning could become an obsession, and not winning left me feeling deep rejection. It was worse when Tracey left school and stopped going to drama classes.

I surged on, cleared all the trophies at one local festival and passed every drama exam with distinction. I was put forward for my ALCM diploma in drama at sixteen, the youngest possible age. I passed the theory with flying colours. To my horror, though, I failed the practical exam and was told I had gone over the top.

I would have given up and gone under at that point but Grandpa was living with us by this time and he taught me a lesson that has lasted me a lifetime. Everyone was stunned by my failure. Grandpa, however, took me to one side and said, "What's your problem, lass? If you don't learn to fail in this life, you're on a dangerous path. Pick yourself up and get going again." So I re-did the exam, feeling ashamed to be entered as a re-sit. I passed, albeit not brilliantly. My passion had gone, but I was beginning to learn not to strive for perfection. That's a lifetime lesson. Perfectionism weaves its way in where insecurity reigns.

Another saving grace in my days after Jonty's loss was a hospital chaplain called Jonathan. Mum and Dad struggled when Annabella left home and Grandpa sold all his property. Mum's depression showed itself in many forms of physical illness. She spent weeks in bed or in hospital, but Jonathan came to visit and invited us to a service in the hospital chapel. He asked Dad to play the electric organ, so Dad went too.

At the start of every service, Jonathan read Psalm 103. It's worth reading often. It spoke to me week after week of God's forgiveness, cleansing, mercy, and love. It also spoke of the healing I wanted for Mum and all the family. Jonathan came to our home one day, a few months after Jonty had gone. I came in from a riding situation which had gone badly wrong. Jonathan showed an interest in my struggle and I felt it was safe to talk as it threw no negative light on my parents. It transpired that Jonathan lived in a village nearby, where he was the vicar. In the village was an Italian gentleman who owned a horse-jumping stable and was from a long line of gifted riders. His faith was important to him, and he attended Jonathan's church when Catholic Mass conflicted with his show-jumping schedule. For a long time, Giovanni had been asking Jonathan to try horse riding. Jonathan had tried, but felt his body and mind weren't designed for it. He suggested I might like an introduction to Giovanni with a view to riding for him, and I agreed wholeheartedly.

> *There's a pattern developing for me as I write. I retell the happy parts easily, and struggle to write what's hard. I don't want to dishonour my parents or be bitter but I do want to be honest. I hope my story will bless and help whoever reads it. Whatever happens, writing it is clarifying and helping me on my journey of understanding with God and is, I think, part of my healing. God never wastes anything.*
>
> *In my depression, when I was twenty-two, God healed a lot of my bitterness towards my parents through a word from James 3:13-17. I asked their forgiveness and felt our family relations improved (see chapter 21) but this was not the whole answer. One of the dangers of "glorious testimony" can be to give a false impression that everything is sorted out in one go rather than being one part of a process. That process is testimony to God's wise working and His goodness, to His care for everyone involved in the battles of life and the wiles of the enemy. At that stage in my life and my family's He brought a degree of harmony and healing and sowed "kingdom seeds". There was, however, a lot more life to be lived. As Matthew 13 describes in the parable of the wheat and the tares, until the right time for harvest God may let both grow together, but He is still protecting the wheat. He's protecting the wheat by leaving the tares in place and not harvesting too soon.*
>
> *Aged fourteen and fifteen I was still living under the care of my parents. In that time God knew Grandpa was about to take radical action. When I was at home aged twenty-two, God knew how to lead us forward. In all the interim years, I believe He was working to grow me and my faith and to keep me safe. He was also caring for my damaged family. There were years, later, when God asked me to break or severely reduce contact with my*

family. That was hard for me and others to understand but we have to keep following God's leading with the knowledge and integrity we have each step of the way.

The enemy weaves complex nets around and between God's children; only God knows the way through. Jesus really is the way, the truth and the life. With Isaiah 50:1-10 firmly in mind I try to follow what Jesus did – to see what God says in the moment and do that even if it doesn't make sense. This ties in with Isaiah 30:15-16 in which Father God invites us to keep returning to Him, and not rush off in our own way, and with verse 21, "...your ears will hear a voice behind you, saying, 'This is the way; walk in it.'"[16]

Over the years God has honed that teaching, and my hearing. He has always led me to helpful elders and mentors who have helped me to check out what I thought He was saying. I love to help others in this way now. It's always about knowing Him and knowing ourselves more and more: "...then I shall know fully, even as I have been fully known."[17] So let's fill in a few details from those messy years after Jonty left.

I did go and ride for Giovanni for the next two years. It was a wonderful experience. In that time, I rode some beautiful horses and even had a jumping lesson from Giovanni himself. The relationship ended suddenly when he moved away. He would have taken me with him, I think, if I'd accepted his offer of caring for his yard while he was away at the Horse of the Year Show, but I made a choice at this point. Care of the yard meant a week off school in my A Level year. Even though I wanted to keep my friendship with Giovanni, I chose to stay at school and maintain my studies. After that, our contact ceased. I was sad, but I'm sure the choice was a good one. Grandpa was living with us then, so with his wonderful guidance, choices like that were easier to make.

---

[16] Isaiah 30:21 (NIV)
[17] 1 Corinthians 13:12 (ESV)

19

Grandpa dies

At seventeen I lost Grandpa. He died peacefully in his sleep at 8.10 a.m. on 23rd February 1969. Before he died he made sure I had received Jesus Christ into my life. He also warned me to go to university as far away from the north as possible so, some time later, I went to a university on the tip of the south coast.

Grandpa had heart failure and bowel cancer, although which one killed him wasn't clear. All I know is that I made him a marmalade sandwich on a Thursday evening, and sat on his bed while he nibbled and chatted. Then he went to sleep and never awoke. The doctor was called to certify his death while I was in school. I came home at lunchtime, still not sure if Grandpa had died, still hoping he hadn't. I was devastated by the news, but was also firmly told I shouldn't be because he wasn't my father. I was told to go back to school and be sure to give my parents the care they needed in their grief.

When Grandpa died, fear and torment grew within me. I was also severely punished for grieving. With Dad and Mum depressed and Annabella unhappy at college, I began to strive to support them, just as I had when I was ten years old. Although I had become a Christian that year, I lost sight of grace. With my grief for Grandpa so heavily repressed, I began to feel evil and would pour all my energy into serving others to feel better. The ritual chanting grew stronger in me, and God's voice was often tuned out.

Grandpa was Dad's father, but Nana, Mum's mother, was also in a hospice dying of cancer at this time. Both my parents were grieving, and with Annabella away at college I was their only carer. I found it hard to manage my A Level studies in those hard days. I couldn't tell anyone how much I missed Grandpa and how frightened I was of life without him.

In fact, I only managed a few days at school. The abuse I suffered had affected my development, and I hadn't grown or entered puberty at the normal time. A couple of years earlier I'd been put on a course of oestrogen tablets to trigger some sort of development. The medication made me very poorly, so with Grandpa's support I'd stopped it as soon as I could. I don't know what really happened in my body after Grandpa died. All I know is that after a few days of compulsory silence I began to cry secretly and my body began to haemorrhage. This lasted for more than two weeks. My mother had to call the GP who put me on bed rest saying the cause was natural grief and emotion. I wasn't allowed to cry in public, but my body seemed to make its own protest.

The time in bed meant I missed my mock A Level exams and fell further behind in my work. A kind biology teacher tried to get me to talk about my grief over Grandpa, but I couldn't; I still felt forbidden to do so.

Nana died during my A Level exams. Little wonder then that on several occasions I had mind blanks and missed out or messed up whole sections of my papers. Our headmistress spent time with me and realised I had issues. She wrote a letter to the Joint Matriculation Board and to my university. Thanks to her intervention, the Board adjusted my grades favourably and the university still offered me a place. I really saw the hand of God in all this. I was even able to encourage my mother that He had a plan for me and was clearly guiding me, and she seemed to hear me and appreciate what I said.

My dad was very lost after Grandpa died, and Mum was disturbed and distressed by the loss of her mother.

> *The death of a close relative carries intense stresses whether the relationship was good or bad. In the case of a bad relationship there may be grief over the problems that existed or the dream of how the relationship might have been.*

Mum threw herself into her teaching. She went back full-time and applied for deputy headships. Dad recovered from a severe heart attack and managed to return to work. He had also become active in Freemasonry, and now he increased his involvement. This gave him opportunity to dine out frequently and to drink heavily. Mum became afraid of him and felt estranged. Later, she would even sometimes phone me from upstairs and asked me to phone Dad, who was downstairs, with messages from her.

> *Division in marriage is a generational curse which has run through our families for several generations. Steve and I were glad to discover we could pray against this so it didn't impact our relationship or our children's. The power of the cross is truly limitless!*

20

Cast out but taken up

My plan had been to train as a veterinary surgeon and I had taken extra courses during my A Levels to gain the correct qualifications, but it became clear I would not reach the required grades. I would have loved to have become a farmer but my parents and teachers thought that was "beneath" me so encouraged me towards nursing. The NHS had devised a new course which would combine academic study for a BSc in Social Admin at a southern university with practical training at a London hospital to become a State Registered Nurse and qualified Health Visitor. The course would take just over five years and graduates were expected to become high flyers in the NHS.

London and the south tied in with Grandpa's advice to study as far away from my parents as possible, so I was pleased to be accepted. There were six of us on the course and it was set to be highly demanding.

Finally, the exciting day came when Dad took me to start my course. My parents had supported Annabella through college financially, taken her on holidays, and been a base to which she could return out of term time. Despite the very different treatment Annabella and I had received at home, I was unprepared for the bombshell that Dad dropped as he left me at the nurses' home in London. He made it very clear that his home was now no longer mine: "That is it now, Helen. You've left home. There is no place for you with us." I was stunned – I had never expected to be banished from my home.

There is a beautiful passage in the Bible in which God describes an abandoned girl child who has been cast out into a field.[18] Girls were not as valuable as boys so an unwanted daughter could be thrown away and left to die. As our society does not countenance that, my parents had to go through the motions with me – the spare child. Instead, my going to university enabled them to cast me out but still maintain their respectability at Rushford.

It is this point that marks the start of my transition into becoming and knowing myself to be a beloved daughter rather than a spare child. This was, sadly, never how my parents saw me, but I started to learn that this is what I am to my Heavenly Father.

> *This is a natural break in my story and in many ways I would be glad to leave it here as it has been so hard to relive these days in writing about them.*
>
> *So let me draw Part One to a close by saying that after being banished so abruptly I struggled to settle into hospital and university life. Years of bitterness followed, of realising that although I had been cast off, I was still bound by emotional and spiritual ties that threatened to destroy me. Yet during those years there were strands of love from Christian people that drew me more closely into healing and life with Jesus to such an extent that I have even been able to become a wife, as God has continued to make me more aware that I am beloved.*
>
> *My hope is that my story will encourage you that, no matter how dark and desperate your present and past may appear, the loving Jesus who drew me to Himself and then into my present fulfilled life is able and willing to love and help and heal you too. He is your perfect friend, help, healer, and shepherd when you allow Him to be Lord and King of your life. It cost Him everything to bring such blessing and salvation to each and every one of us, His beloved children.*

---

[18] See Ezekiel 16:9ff

Part One

PART TWO

I would like to pause the year-by-year telling of my story here and over the next three chapters explore some treasures from God that helped me into my deeper healing and to encourage anyone struggling through depression or lengthy deep healing.

God never fails or leaves us.

Part Two

21

First breakdown

I experienced my first period of depression while studying at university. While I had no outside help, God spoke very clearly to me. I had time and space to press into Him and that's what I did. During that time, my parents took me into their home, probably because the university contacted them, assuming that I would still have a home there. In an old school notebook, I wrote pages and pages expressing my feelings and anger. At that stage, all my writing came from feeling dreadful about myself. I cried to God for help to change, and He began that journey, although it has taken years and years.

> *Sometimes healing isn't an instant miracle, but it is a miracle nonetheless. That's why I'm persevering with this book. It's helping me to see God's hand even in the darkest times. My hope and prayer is that it will encourage others to keep following Him even when the light seems a pinprick as I described in my very early years of life. His light dispels the darkness, however small that light seems in the beginning.*

By the time I was twenty-two, I had lived eight years in growing bitterness, trying so hard not to harm or dishonour my parents in anything I said, but turning my anger in on myself. Some relief came when I was sent home from university and left with my bewildered family to "recover". All I had was God and a single visit to the local GP. In that visit, however, I somehow managed to tell the doctor that I didn't want my parents to feel they had done anything wrong. I felt I'd failed them by not managing university well, and in fact in all the other exams I'd taken since Jonty left. The GP wisely said, "I'm not sure we get it right or wrong as parents. We just do the best we can." That was a lifeline for me. It freed me from worries that I was wrongly putting blame on my parents. Acknowledging my perceptions had validity for my healing, as I realised the only person I could judge or change was myself. So I came to God and simply said, "I can't change or judge my parents, so please show me what I can change in my attitude and what I can do to bridge the chasm between us."

God immediately led me to James 3 and Hebrews 12. In Hebrews we learn about a root of bitterness that can spring up and cause trouble if we fail to obtain God's grace. That bitterness can "defile many"[19]. I could see I was unhappy in all my relationships, both at home with my family and at university.

James 3:15 describes bitter jealousy and selfish ambition as being "earthly, unspiritual, demonic"[20] and James 4 shows how God gives us grace (verse 6) to resist the devil (verse 7) and to come close to Him (verse 8). All I knew was that I needed His grace and His closeness and I would do anything to find it again. I had not known it since Grandpa had died. I felt I needed to have an honest conversation with my parents, but I didn't know how to start. I asked God to open the way very clearly if this conversation was to take place.

I went downstairs and asked my mother if we could talk. Mum, Dad and my sister were all struggling with depression, and my return from university was an added concern. They'd always hoped I was destined for great things because somewhere inside me there used to be, in their words, a "very good brain" and a "strong, charming personality". Mum was unsure what to say, so I asked her what was upsetting her about me. Her reply, "I don't understand why you're so bitter and jealous," used the exact words I'd read in James 3 and Hebrews 12. I didn't need to argue my case. All I needed to do was stand against the enemy. So I agreed with her and shared the scriptures with her and asked for her forgiveness. She wept and so did I. She called Dad into the room and we were all able to talk together.

There was much more healing, understanding, and unravelling to be done in each of our lives, but that day a kingdom seed was sown and

---

[19] Hebrews 12:15 (NIV)
[20] James 3:15 (ESV)

the enemy's hold began to be loosened – all through two verses of Scripture and God's faithfulness to answer when we call.

> *This illustrates a principle we have discovered to be a means of breakthrough in relationship difficulties for clients as well as ourselves: "Go low." Rather than focusing on the pain of the situation or where the other person is wrong, and waiting for them to take the first step, ask Jesus if there is any way in which you have contributed to the rift. If He shows you something, deal with it with Him and, when you are sorted with Jesus, go to the other, own your fault, and ask their forgiveness. Even if, as in one situation we experienced, you feel the blame burden is very largely theirs and only slightly yours, "going low" in this way is very effective. At the very least you are at peace with yourself and with Jesus. Very often reconciliation will come too, although not always. The other person may not be prepared to acknowledge their fault so you cannot be reconciled in that area, although you can relate in others. This was the case with my dad. I forgave him but he refused to allow me to tell him my perspective, and that meant that our relationship was not as close as I would have liked, but it was still close enough for him to hear the gospel from Steve and become a Christian in the months before his death.*

The chapter went on, giving me a recipe for recognising God's wisdom over and above my own: "The wisdom from above is first pure, then peaceable, gentle, open to reason, full of mercy and good fruits, without uncertainty or insincerity and the harvest of righteousness is sown in peace by those who make peace."[21]

> *There was much more healing and releasing and learning to be done. I made many more mistakes and bad choices in my life. So did my parents and sister. Don't we all?*

I believe that from that day God had a greater foothold in my family. Annabella and Mum started attending the church where I'd gone in my teenage years, and joined a Basic Christianity course. Dad went along too from time to time but he was confused between church teaching and the Bible they used, and the Masonic Bible and teaching

---

[21] James 3:17-18 (RSV)

which was very different. Grandpa had never allowed Dad to join the Freemasons. He didn't feel it was a healthy group for a Christian to join. When Grandpa died, however, Dad did join. He believed they would give his family security and I think it gave him a sense of belonging when he missed the village and the rituals so much.

Annabella and Mum made some sort of commitment to Jesus Christ quite soon after God began to heal our family relationships.

> *I say this with apprehension. Those who have known me in the last forty years of my life may well think that my family relationships looked extremely unhealed. The key point, however, is that I had begun to learn to seek God and His will and leading over and above anything else I was being told. I've needed to grow a lot in discernment, but that anchor of having Jesus Christ as my foundation[22], and being able to draw on His wisdom[23], has never failed me.*

---

[22] See 1 Corinthians 3
[23] See James 3:17

22

Second breakdown

> *I'm fascinated by how God keeps and protects and enables us until His perfect time for just enough healing as He knows best. Mourning Grandpa has come in stages for me. The mourning of serious losses needs to do that.*

When I was a twenty-five-year-old health visitor I experienced my second major breakdown. My health visiting patch was tough, and that and other aspects of my life contributed to a burden of stress which had been increasing in spite of – or even because of – the ways I tried to cope.

My GP at university had sent me to numerous specialists who performed several investigative operations and examinations. All these were in very personal and private places. On several occasions groups of medical students were present, although no permission had been asked of me. A sheet designed to cover me was removed for examination. By the end of all this I could identify strongly with the woman with the haemorrhage in the Bible[24] who suffered for twelve years and spent all her money on trying to get better. Those days were hard for me and my job was in jeopardy. My sick pay was about to be reduced because of the frequent long periods I had to take off work.

The gynaecologists and rectal surgeons who examined me came to a strange and revealing conclusion: that my symptoms were due to damage inexplicably caused to those parts of my body, extreme stress and "complex family ties".

---

[24] See Mark 5:24-35

The GP had been very kind to me and even continued to see me after his retirement. When he died of cancer I felt devastated. Not long after this I received my diagnosis and asked a friend to find out if I could register with her Christian GP. He agreed and by the grace of God he was in place and able to support me when I finally broke down. We may not always realise how much God is at work in our lives. I certainly didn't at the time, but hindsight is a wonderful thing.

This GP introduced me to his church. It was Anglican, which helped me feel secure as I knew the service would start at 6:30 p.m. and end after the sermon, a few prayers and the blessing. However, I never wanted to be seen and their way of praying for people really frightened me. I also began to shake when they prayed "Holy Spirit, come" prayers, or offered communion. I'd ceased to use Grandpa's little book *A Companion to Communion;* it was too painful for me now he'd died. To counter this, I developed a good working plan. I'd arrive at church after the start, at 6.35 p.m. or later, sit at the back near the open doors, and leave after the sermon. I never took communion in those dark days, but I heard the Word of God beautifully taught and I sensed His love through that Spirit-filled congregation. The Christian GP was highly embarrassed eighteen months later when he asked where I went to church. When I told him I went to the same church as him he was astonished, but actually it was evidence of my careful plans to stay hidden and still seek God as best I could.

In my job as a health visitor I came across some difficult issues which I hadn't learned to handle in a healthy manner. I worked with one family, alongside a child psychologist. Tragically, the children had been playing with matches and caused a house fire in which one of them died. I'd arrived at their house on a routine visit to find medics, firemen, and police still at work.

Soon after, another tragedy occurred involving the death of a baby. The child's mother didn't speak English. She was a foreign single mum whose relatives had abandoned her when she became pregnant. Somehow, and for reasons no one could ascertain, she had travelled to England. Her antenatal care was lacking, so I was asked to visit. We developed a trusting relationship and found ways of communicating; I loved this sort of work. When the baby was born her joy was obvious. A family had offered her a room and all seemed well. While I was picking up the pieces of the family devastated by the house fire, a call came from my nursing officer. The foreign mum had lost her baby. He had died in the night and no one knew the cause. I was devastated. With hindsight, I suspect I'd bought into this mother's sense of abandonment.

Both families knew tragedy and loss at a deep level. With my own unhealed loss and trauma, I was in no position to help either family. I grew increasingly tense, guilty, and depressed. I started to lose weight and exercise more and more, even though I was ill and exhausted. I bought a book of exercises designed for Army cadets and pummelled my body as I wrongly believed Paul's letters advocated.[25] I grew distant from God, feeling evil.

I now recognise this was an echo of how I'd felt as a child.

All I wanted to do was hide, close down and – if I could find the courage – die. I felt guilty for my thoughts of suicide, so starving myself seemed better. It was strangely more in God's hands, whoever God was. I tried to keep reading the Bible as Grandpa had taught me. I tried praying but felt too evil. I now arose around 5.30 a.m. to try to wrestle with my body and spirit for two to three hours so I could do my work better. I felt a failure in every way.

In the February of that year a lovely young lady came to lodge with us for two weeks. Her father was an evangelist in the Italian villages. She sang and danced for him when he preached, and had a bond with him which reminded me of mine with Grandpa. She had a love for God as her Father, which broke my heart, although I can't even remember her name or why she came to us. She soon went home to Italy. I wonder if God sent her for me, as in the short time she was with us she opened my heart to submit to His love again.

When I was reading my Bible, a verse caught my attention, which described iniquity as being like "a breach in a high wall, cracked and bulging, that collapses suddenly"[26]. This spoke deeply into my soul. I knew there was something very wrong inside me and I needed to do something about it or I'd collapse beyond repair. The end of the next verse referred to a potter's vessel smashed beyond repair. Just as I had when I was thirteen years old, I heard God, almost audibly, saying, "You need to stop striving and let Me in to help, My way." That day

---

[25] A misinterpretation of 1 Corinthians 9:27
[26] Isaiah 30:13 (NIV)

could have been my point of collapse, but in truth it was my day of salvation.

I asked forgiveness for striving and prayed He'd deliver me fully from whatever iniquity was dwelling inside me. I'd no idea how long the journey would be or how on earth He'd help me travel it, but He has been, and continues to be, faithful every step of the way.

As I drove into work I had a sense of God's presence. I'd known this in times with Grandpa, one night at my aunt and uncle's when I'd called out to Him aged just five years old, and that night when He'd made me see He'd given me Jonty on the exact day I'd asked, 19th May 1966. I parked my car, walked into the clinic, and began to shake from deep inside. I couldn't see clearly. I felt lightheaded and very dizzy. My friend, the clinic assistant, asked me if I was all right. I said yes but my shaking increased. I was terrified. The other health visitors encouraged me into a back room; their kindness was overwhelming. A scream of pain, fear, and anguish came from deep inside me and my sobbing was uncontrollable. I don't know how long it lasted, but once I could utter any words, all I could say was "Grandpa's died" over and over again. Understandably, everyone thought my Grandpa had died that day, but in reality, eight years had passed since his death. When I was able to talk more, I couldn't make sense of my feelings at all. Dad had fairly recently had a heart attack so I tried to relate my strange reactions to that.

My colleagues and superiors were all medically trained so they had the sense to send me to my Christian GP. Able to hear God and tune in to the Holy Spirit, he had a lovely lightness and sense of humour. Realising how fragile I was, he saw me weekly for the first few weeks, for a double twenty-minute session. These were booked at the end of the day so we could go overtime if necessary. For the first time ever, I had time and space to talk about my struggles with both life and faith.

23

Recovery begins

All I knew in those early weeks was deep darkness and despair. I would write to God about it, but I received no response. My days were filled with crying – sometimes for two hours at a time – intense anger, jealousy, and shaking. I had horrendous sexual flashbacks and serious physical and sexual pain.

I would take the Bible passages explored in the service on a Sunday and ask God to expand on them through the week. In the safety of my secret place with Him, I began to hear His voice again. I received comfort through the scriptures, but was unable to get far beyond feeling evil about my anger, jealousy, and dark, sexual thoughts and feelings. None of it made sense, but I knew He was there and had been kind and caring enough to hear my prayer for a horse and to keep Grandpa at peace in long periods of pain and sickness.

One Sunday the vicar preached on Psalm 22. He called it the "Goat Psalm" because it was "full of buts"! It spoke deep into my soul of someone feeling dark and desperate, alone and abandoned, and full of doubt and questions. The vicar said that there was someone in the congregation who related to Jesus on the cross. It opened hope for me that Jesus might understand me and could possibly find help for me, a revelation which came to me as the vicar was preaching. When it hit me I shook, became short of breath, and wanted to scream, so I left the church. I kept reading the psalm through the week, but it had the same effect, so I reduced it to a short prayer: "God, if You do care, please lead me to people who can help me."

A while later I found a book at the back of church written by a Christian consultant psychologist. She explained how things that have happened to us can hurt us. Feelings can be repressed and cause us to feel physically ill. She described some of my symptoms as the manifestations of such an illness. She suggested anyone with these symptoms should seek medical help. I asked my GP about the book and found that, unbelievably, he had already referred me to this very consultant. Help was on its way. God had heard me and acted – again!

Before I could see the consultant, I had a pile of forms to complete. They asked questions about my past, my current condition, and my family and other relationships. Simply filling in the forms was cathartic.

> *We often employ a similar practice for people who come to see us.*

I cried for days and wasn't sure I wanted to see the specialist as I was afraid of what she might deduce. Speaking to people outside my family was always forbidden.

Mercifully, I managed to make it to my appointment. It was over an hour long but the specialist was delightful. She realised I was fragile and terrified of talking about myself and my upbringing. I didn't know why I was so disturbed. The consultant concluded that I clearly needed help and that I was far too fragile to be able to cope in a therapy group. Amazingly, she offered me individual therapy for ten months, at that time the longest period possible. An interesting requirement was that I should be back at work before therapy commenced. This was so that I didn't become so engrossed in my past and my feelings that I couldn't continue to relate to normal life. Whatever had caused my problems was in the past. I had survived. I could now learn about the effects of my past and choose to heal and to live differently.

With this new hope in place I was eventually able to return to work. The consultant wisely pointed out that the place of prayer in my current condition would be simply for other people to uphold me. I needed healing emotionally in order to become more balanced in my faith. She did, however, encourage me to continue to see my precious friend and mentor, Georgia. Georgia spent an hour a week with me, encouraging me to hear what God had to say to me through the psalms and other scriptures. She also helped me to balance any wayward thoughts and discern more carefully the voice of God.

Georgia had herself been rescued from a horrendous past. Her story was embodied in Psalm 31, a psalm that gave me great hope.

So I went back to work. It was exhausting at first and I needed to limit everything else I did. I had been very involved in a discipleship ministry, but sadly all the support I received from them fell away when I was no longer able to serve them. I am now able to understand their thinking, but at the time it was very painful. I felt rejected, and developed a sense of having to be useful to God and his people or I'd be thrown out. That belief was also reinforced by my past, in which I'd felt I had to serve the family, or be disowned and rejected. My discipleship group was also suspicious of people who talked about feelings and weakness. Mental illness frightens many people – a sad fact that is true, even today.

> *I'm finding this time of deep soul pain and confusion really hard to write. My head and body still ache when I recall these sad, dark days.*

These difficult times seemed endless and hope was just a pinprick of light on a distant horizon, but it was there. My hope was in God, whoever He was. I knew He was there because He'd answered two very significant prayers. He'd brought me Jonty and He'd led me to this lovely consultant. I also had Georgia faithfully encouraging me. Often ill and housebound, she had been so damaged in her past that she now needed regular injections to keep her alive. She had been able to forgive her abusers and she found God to be her closest friend and Saviour. She always had time for me, and encouraged me – whatever happened – that God loved me and that I wasn't evil.

Georgia's encouragement was vital. There were points during this time when darkness would fall upon me, usually when I was in church or praying alone. The darkness spoke of suicide and torment and terror happening to me and my family. It overwhelmed me so I would scream and shake and often fall to the ground. Perplexed onlookers would call for medical help and often politely asked for me to be removed, either from the church or from my lodgings, when this phenomenon occurred. I was as frightened as they were, but being "removed" was hard. Georgia would take me into her home, but could never let me live permanently with her. She was a well-known speaker and minister and often had to go away, or have key people to stay with her. This was, in fact, healthy for me. I needed to keep boundaries between my everyday life and the problems I was seeking to work through. My Christian GP was wonderful in giving me helpful support, medication, and also in advising my frightened friends how to manage me without becoming overwhelmed.

I needed a team of supporters. No one person could have managed someone in my serious condition. I am really grateful to all who ventured to offer what they could to keep me alive and making progress. In my worst moments I was jealous, angry, frightened, and confused. Manipulation was a dangerous behaviour I could fall into in my desperate state. Caring friends needed to be able to keep boundaries so that I didn't burden them to burnout.

> *Steve and I now teach churches how best to manage people in the condition I was in at that time. It's a place of battle. The enemy, emotions, beliefs, and deep wounds all have serious sway. Church teams can become divided, discouraged, and exhausted if someone like I was comes into the congregation. If my caring team hadn't been so wise and loving, I would not be where I am today – in fact, I may well not still be alive.*

Eventually, I began my appointments with the therapist at the main hospital.

> *With hindsight and my current expertise, I'd say he practised psychodynamic therapy. This is a therapy that looks at difficulties in relationships with special reference to childhood experiences. As in several other methods of therapy, there can be long periods of silence as a therapist seeks to encourage the client to discover and express his or her feelings.*

It was excruciating, but strangely helpful. From a very early age I had been heavily programmed to repress my feelings and respond to instructions. My attempts to follow my own thoughts and desires had resulted in serious punishment.

This therapist, John, started by asking a few open questions.

> *Open questions are a counsellor's stock in trade. They invite an answer that draws out the client's own perceptions. Their main characteristic is that they make a yes or no answer impossible. Who, where, when, what, and how are helpful words to use in an open question.*

John often asked, "And how did you feel?" That question filled me with fear and unpleasant bodily reactions. I had been trained to be "unselfish" and not consider my own feelings. My poor relatives lived the same way; that's how they'd ended up in the claws of ritual.

> *Self-awareness is a key to managing our thinking. In Paul's words, we need "to take captive every thought to make it obedient to Christ"[27]. To bring our thinking into line with God's will and thoughts, we need to know what we think. Psalm 139 tells us that God not only knows our thoughts, but He understands them as well. In recent years, with the help of good secular training and prayer ministry, I've learned to come to God and let Him help me know what I think and tell me what to do with those thoughts.*

Those first therapy sessions opened the door to the knowledge that I had feelings. After over a year of therapy, I began to feel I had permission to discover and express those feelings when I was with John. In fact, it was the only way to get through a session. I learned this after several fifty-minute "therapeutic hours" in which John had asked his question, or even said absolutely nothing. Afraid to speak because I couldn't discover what was required of me – the rules again – I had also remained in awkward silence for the whole hour.

God helped me through the scriptures. In the psalms, I saw David expressing emotion. In Corinthians, Proverbs, Jeremiah and James, Hosea and Isaiah, I learned that the Holy Spirit knows and feels our emotions and thoughts. What we think affects how we feel, something I learned much later in life and therapy. Since God seemed to allow feelings, I began to write pages and pages of feelings as prayers to Him in my journal. I was passionate to walk in integrity and to learn truth in my inward being, because that was what God seemed to want.

This brought great release in these early days as God spoke powerfully through Scripture. I bought a series of books called *Search the Scriptures,* with Bible study questions on every book in the Bible. The course took three years and I loved it, and somehow learned to ask God His thoughts when I got stuck for an answer. I now see that that was being prophetic – I just didn't know it was called that! I didn't learn to ask God's response in a prophetic sense until decades later.

---

[27] 2 Corinthians 10:5 (NIV)

Nowadays, in our ministry, Steve and I encourage clients to make a habit of asking God's response after they've expressed their feelings. He is the God of all comfort. His response is always in truth and love. I think I learned this best when our first child died. John came to visit me in my home when that tragedy happened. He was clear that it was strictly against all the rules, but it meant the world to Steve and me. It confirmed that John really cared about me as a person and that he wasn't just pushing me through a model of therapy. Boundaries are very important in therapy and prayer ministry, but so is genuine love. I believe God led John to break a few boundaries to help me survive the tragic death of our son Joe.

Love and care for each individual client is one of our highest values in Bespoke. Steve and I seek to stay open to God's leading whilst adhering to wise boundaries. Sometimes it is a difficult path to discern, but God is faithful and can cover mistakes in our faltering steps. That knowledge gives me faith to seek and follow His leading as best I can.

PART THREE

Part Three

24

Further healing

Let's return now to the year-by-year telling of my story and the start of my university studies. By the grace of God, I gained a place on a pioneering new degree course: a BSc in Social Admin with SRN and Health Visitor qualifications.

> *I so value the kind, generous help of friends and family in helping me to pull my story together. Without them I would have given up long ago. I feel a bit like Moses: God called me to write, but I struggled for years; it never seemed to come together; then He showed me how to write with His help, and added more invaluable support when I felt too weak to carry on, just as He gave Aaron to Moses and then added Jethro and other leaders, Joshua and Caleb. We need Him always and we need each other. Thank you, lovely friends and family. I love you all so, so much. You make me smile, and as for God... well... you are A-M-A-Z-I-N-G!*
>
> *I've been asked to extend the telling of my story in Part One to the age of twenty-five. I'm going back to my former way of writing to do this – that is, to set aside thirty minutes a day and ask the Holy Spirit to help me write as He wants. Clearly, some of the writing is me and marred by my own thinking, but hearing God is like that. In being open to reason from others (James 3:17) I trust that greater clarity comes to what I felt I heard God say. James 3:13-18 has been a precious help to me since my first breakdown and depression. I needed to know how to have greater confidence that I was hearing His voice.*

> *It's a mark of my ongoing healing that I can now entertain this exercise. Last year I couldn't even face thinking about life after I left home. It was all a blur of pain and memories were blocked. Now, clarity is coming.*

Had my father not rejected me so blatantly when I started the course, I may have had a better chance of survival. As it was, his telling me that I was now wholly on my own raised old fears of being away from home, which tapped into my experiences as a five-year-old at my aunt and uncle's house and my subsequent disowning and dishonouring by my father.

The first four weeks of my degree course were in the London hospital. We had accommodation in a nurses' home. My most significant memory is that there was a print of a horse on my chair cover. God often encouraged me – and still does – that it's really Him speaking when I have pictures or visions relating to horses. This horse-print kept me confident that God was still with me. I felt totally abandoned and alone except for this reassurance of His presence. All I remember of my first night of the course is sitting on the horse-print chair weeping and crying out to God for His help and for at least a few people to help me to keep following Him.

I realise now that I was still missing Grandpa. Because I had not been allowed to grieve his death, repressed grief became an issue for me. After my messy A Level exams and a summer full of the stress of my mother's mother dying, I landed in London already bewildered, lost, and stressed, when Dad rendered his final blow of abandonment.

For the first two weeks of my month in London I suffered panic attacks and a strange dizziness and light-headedness. I managed everything we were asked to do, probably because it was largely a month of observation and orientation. As there were only six of us on the course, social demands were minimal. I don't recall much social activity with the other girls. I can't even remember if they lived close. I suspect we were actually all in the same nurses' home, but with my high-level stress all I remember is surviving a day, running to my room at night, and creeping down to the swimming pool in the basement very late at night when I knew I'd be alone. I'm not sure we were allowed to swim alone, but I needed to expend my nervous energy so I'd pray for protection and privacy and swim anyway.

About two weeks into the course, my prayer for help was answered. I was the only Christian of the six of us so I quietly sought God on my own each evening. We six were together in the hospital dining room one Friday afternoon when a senior charge nurse called Maddy approached us. I was initially intimidated but she was lovely, full of bounce and smiles. She asked if any of us fancied ice cream. We all said, "Yes!" Ice cream and good company were being offered by a Christian nurses' ministry, and three or four of us joined Maddy and her friends for ice cream in St James' Park the following Sunday afternoon. They were really friendly and told us about their group, their church, and their shared love for Jesus. I was over the moon. God had heard my prayer, and two of my colleagues also showed some interest.

Maddy arranged to meet us in the dining room the following Friday. At this meeting, she invited us to a nurses' tea, followed by church if we fancied. My friends weren't keen on church and I don't remember going. I think I felt safer coming home with them than being left alone. Maddy did tell us about the service in the nurses' home chapel, which I did attend. It was quiet, like the old eight o'clock communion I'd known at home. It only lasted forty minutes, which was long enough for me in my stressed state. Much of the ritual training was proving a battleground in my mind and body. The enemy is cruel. When we are weak he presses in; but God is so much greater and ever faithful. With Maddy, the chapel services, and alone with God in my room, I kept finding oases of peace, which is how I survived the first four weeks of my degree – purely by the grace of God and the obedience of His faithful people. I was learning that people like Grandpa do exist in the outside world and His peace and help is accessible even when the enemy presses in from without and within.

25

The move to university in the south

Here I go again! It's taken me all day so far to get to my half-hour of writing. I forgot how disturbing my story is. The years at university and nurse training are ones I've chosen never to review – probably because they were so hard.

We six students were put into lodgings at university to keep us focused on work and out of mischief. We were seen as something special by the nursing and health visiting departments, but the university students weren't so keen, and keeping us separate in this way was unhealthy for our social adjustment. Some of our six were in lodgings with other regular students, which helped them mix in with university life.

I, however, was placed with a family who had a teenage daughter and no other children. I think the parents were older than usual, so more children had been out of the question, and their daughter was lonely. Her experience of life was totally unlike mine, and we were poles apart. She attended private senior school, was used to a high society social life, and was kept in cotton wool by her doting parents. The student who had lodged with them the previous year had bonded closely with her; I suspect they were from more similar roots. I was in no state to befriend her, which is what her parents wanted me to do. Needless to say, I did want to try to please them, but it was a huge pressure on my arrival at university. For a start, having to eat breakfast with the mother and be home for high tea at 4.30 p.m. and an evening meal at 7.30 p.m. made any life at university virtually impossible. In addition, the house was a distance from the campus. The family wanted to live well away from the student areas, and their estate was beautiful but deadly boring and lonely.

Between or after meals and at weekends there was an unspoken but clear expectation that I would spend time with the daughter. We were given various activities to do together. I hated them all and she was clearly disappointed in me.

> *Yesterday was a Sunday and we are on holiday. I took the day off writing. My excuse was that I needed a Sabbath but I'm aware I'd actually only written two half-hours all that week. On further reflection, I realise I struggle to recall these university years because they are largely unhealed. I have had lots of ministry into my childhood traumas. The years following seemed less important as we were seeking to heal the roots of my issues. Sometimes, however, the fruits and consequences of those root events also need healing. In the early years of life, we learn patterns that help us to cope with future traumas and trials. These patterns create ways of being and behaving that can cause us more trauma if we are living as the world has moulded us rather than in the truth of how God intended us to be. Steve writes about this in his book, "Closer to Jesus". Writing about the years from eighteen to twenty-five and recalling what happened opens fears in me that I will have to work through more painful memories. That is never an easy thing to do, but now I know that the resulting healing and freedom and experience of God's loving presence are well worth the brief pain of the memory. He only ever asks us to touch into past pain to the level necessary for us to bring it to the cross and receive His healing grace.*
>
> *What I said about patterns laid down in early childhood is particularly significant in my time at university. In my first year, for example, I was firmly entrenched in the belief that I had to do what those in authority required. My childhood program-ming meant that I saw having food and a roof over my head as a reward. This put my host family in authority, according to my thinking, so I forced myself to comply with their requirements of me; I so wanted to be a good student for them.*
>
> *This thinking was mixed up with religion, which often happens in emotionally vulnerable adults. I was extremely*

worried that my family may not have accepted Jesus, which the Christian Union believed was necessary for salvation. I was terrified that if the world ended it would be too late for them and we would be separated for ever. As such, I felt responsible for their happiness and safety. I'm sure the enemy spots the emotionally weak and is attracted to them. He is out to steal, kill, and destroy God's beloved children.

In the year leading to the beginning of my course, a friend who had been paramount in leading me to Jesus and His forgiveness and grace was killed in a car accident along with her mother, recently married pregnant sister, and her beloved new puppy. These experiences left me afraid of death and opened up many childhood fears in which I had been programmed to believe God was frightening and wouldn't rescue me if I ever felt I was going to die. I was struggling emotionally with complex grief, and physically and cognitively with serious dark programming and body memories. I was also exhausted because these memories came in night terrors, and the struggles of university left me anxious all day and performing poorly.

In Freshers' Week, I was introduced to the Christian Union, which had a strong evangelistic bent, based on proclaiming human sinfulness and our need for Jesus Christ's salvation. Another Christian declared that the end of the world was close. I became so disturbed in the first weeks of my time at university that I became unwell. Despite my father's abandonment, I begged my parents to let me go home after three weeks in the south. The journey took six hours, so the weekend at home was very short, but I didn't care. I was obsessed with the need to tell my family that the end of the world was near and that they needed to accept Jesus before that crisis occurred. My visit and my news were badly received and my parents sent me swiftly back to university and rang my tutors to complain about the Christian organisations. My father had a mantra he used with anyone in authority over me. He would explain how my mother had grown up in a children's home, and how he therefore had become her carer to help her with her mental instabilities. He would tell people that I, sadly, had inherited my mother's mental and emotional weaknesses. My tutors and landlady (Dad had spoken to her as well) now only tightened their strict boundaries on how I should live at university. All this made relating to my peers extremely difficult.

Deep inside, by the grace of God and of Grandpa, I didn't believe that I was as unstable as my father wanted people to believe. I was loath to dishonour him or my mother, but Grandpa had helped me to acknowledge that some of the ways and thoughts forced upon me in childhood were not healthy. He taught me to forgive those who damaged me, and to adhere to Jesus' teaching which I could find in God's Word. So, trapped in my digs and tormented by night terrors, I spent many hours reading the Bible any way I could and calling out to God for help.

He is so faithful. In my fourth week at university one of my peers, who was housed with a lovely, lively Christian couple, invited me to church and to a meal with another Christian group. This colleague had committed her life to Christ early that month, and her enthusiasm and joy in God and His people inspired me to hope again. In Theresa and her Christian friends, I met again that beautiful "Something" or "Someone" who had lived and loved me through Grandpa.

The Christian group loved and valued me. We had fun together over meals, playing outdoor games, learning to study and memorise the Bible, attending church and even going away to weekend conferences.

My parents were concerned. My landlady was unhappy. My tutors wanted to challenge me, but I was finding a peace beyond understanding. I was beginning to shine in all my practical and academic work, so no one could really complain. How great is our God! "How beautiful are the feet of those who bring good news"[28] to people like Theresa and me. I was being saved, protected, and rescued all over again. I'm sure this was in response to Grandpa's many prayers for me, and of course to the grace and love of the "hound of heaven", my searching shepherd.

This Christian group offered a "buddy" to come alongside individual students and help us grow in discipleship and in our walk with Jesus. This was offered but not forced on us. I readily accepted and was introduced to a lovely lady in her late twenties called Amy.

> *Back to writing again. It's later in the day because I have just spent time chatting to my sister. She is currently struggling through chemotherapy to combat severe pancreatic cancer. I'm anxious that this book could seem negative towards my sister*

---

[28] Romans 10:15

and my parents. One of my biggest barriers to ever talking about my struggles in life has been my learned unease with complaint and grumbling, which were never allowed in my childhood years.

In my first year after university, I took a job in paediatrics to increase my confidence as a senior nurse. I never felt the two-year accelerated graduate training gave enough ward management experience. That year was hard, but my sister visited me and we began to want to be friends. She became a Christian and over the years we have both matured and mellowed. Now I can't face the thought of losing her. My parents also came to know Jesus and, by the enormous grace of God and my long-suffering husband, we managed to maintain a level of relationship that had some very precious moments.

My biggest breakthrough came when I was well into my fifties. Steve and I were leading Alpha and discipleship groups, and our children had flown the nest. In a Holy Spirit ministry time, God spoke to me about a ceiling on my experience of Him. On retreat a while later, He said that while I could stay in this position and be fruitful, He also wanted to invite me to go deeper with Him. This, He promised, would be even more fruitful. It came with an honest image that this would feel to me like the woman with the jar of expensive anointing oil, or the widow giving her last mite, or the woman with Elijah giving away her last meal.

I couldn't resist His invitation and sought ministry as He directed. Breakthrough took over eighteen months of long, almost weekly prayer sessions. The first few weeks were a major struggle because detailed memories arose concerning all my ritual training and experiences. The demonic influence in me was strong. One day, about three weeks in, my minister and senior counsellor encouraged me to speak out what I was hiding, saying that my perception was my perception and needed to come into God's light. It was not anyone's place to judge what my heart and body and mind knew. So I began to speak out in those sessions and the dam of evil burst and was drained. God showed us that very picture: that Steve and I were a dam on the evil past, so that it didn't flow down to future generations. Instead, the flow was the sweet water of His Holy Spirit.

Generational blessing is real and what thrills my heart is that even my parents and sister eventually tasted His blessing. His heart is for total redemption!

So now I'm back to writing with confidence that as you read this book you will understand it as my perception of my life. I do not want to sow any seeds of bitterness or put myself in the place of judgement. I simply want to help people to find Him, however impossible this feels. Bring how you see things to God and let Him lead you forward to freedom in a right and proper way.

It's taken the full half-hour of writing to say all I've just said so I think I'm going to leave it here for now. I'm saddened by grief for my sister and in no fit place to encounter my past. It has been good to celebrate God's healing grace today. I will continue my story tomorrow or later today – however He leads me.

At first, Amy seemed quiet and diffident but she was actually beautifully strong and determined in her own quiet way. She wanted to take me out for a meal to have our first get-to-know-you session. This presented me with a dilemma because I'd been asked to be at home for meals with my host family. Their strange demand soon became evident to Amy and the Christian group, who encouraged me to see that student life could embrace an element of freedom to form one's own opinions and ways of living. This was hampered not only by my host family's restrictions, but also by edicts from my tutors and parents that I was simply to study and not to attend any Christian group meetings; they said I was too unstable. It was with the group, however, that I was finding peace. Theresa and my new Christian friends encouraged me to challenge these restrictions and to begin to make some of my own choices. I saw the sense in this and eventually asked my host family to release me to take bed and breakfast only. I thought they might send me away, but they were able to accept that their demands had hindered my ways of working and studying. Once released to eat on campus or with friends, I could frequent the library and work there much more easily.

Amy helped me to make the initial break by collecting me in her car to attend meetings. She called at the house and charmed my landlord and landlady with her professionalism and lovely nature. They valued her maturity and that she held a very good steady job.

As Amy's friendship and the group teaching gave me increasing peace and personal security, my work improved greatly. No one could complain in the face of the healthy results I was achieving. I was learning to face a degree of cost in obedience to Jesus and reaping the rewards of obedience. God is no man's debtor. Guided Bible time and teaching about God's brilliant way of living was freeing me to question some of the ways I had been taught as a child.

> There's an exercise I love to offer clients. It looks at various life situations and invites them to write the first thing that they believe their mum, dad or a significant other might say about that situation. Then I ask them to write their personal belief at gut level. With Christians I often add, "...and now ask God what He thinks about this." Freedom and maturity are found in forming our own beliefs about matters and realising how often we simply move along in what others have told us, often not understanding why they do what they do. For example, we always boiled all our drinking water in Grandma's house. This came from her fear that water contamination had killed her daughter. Nowadays there is no need to boil water but it took my parents a long, long time to stop boiling water even in a modern house.

My first year at university got better and better. I had occasional night terrors, but found that I could find peace again if I recited my newly-learned Bible verses. At the end of the year I agreed to go away on a Christian conference. My parents had now decided that I needed to be at home every holiday – such a turnaround from what Dad had said in London! I think discussion with my tutors had opened them to the idea that students generally went home in the holidays. My parents had reached college age during the war years. Despite their interest in education, they were therefore unable to go to university, and I was the first family member to attend, so I feel my parents can be forgiven for not understanding how it all worked. I also sense they wanted greater control over my life and saw opportunity in having me home for long holidays. Asking to go away to a conference was, therefore, a major cause of disagreement and opposition. I was, however, learning to be determined in certain matters, especially where obedience to God was concerned.

This determination stayed with me through the following years of my degree. My second and third years were spent in London with a set of university graduates training as nurses. There were twenty-two in the group and several were mature Christians. The hospital also maintained a strong Christian base so we had prayers every morning and evening on the wards. In study weeks, Christian students from our group led a longer prayer time; I was in my element!

I started life in the nurses' home. Quite quickly, nurses who were members of the same Christian group as Amy and my university friends came to visit me and we bonded immediately. One of the members of this group joined the nursing course. Fiona was in her early thirties and is a special friend even today. Not long into the course I found myself living in a beautiful London flat with Fiona and several other Christians who were already in professional jobs.

It was costly for me to be associated with this group. My family was angry and my university tutors expressed concern, but two of my nursing tutors were very committed Christians and the third, Penny, was led to Jesus by Fiona. They became close friends. To accelerate our learning, the six of us doing the five-year degree course received extra tutoring, and two of the tutors worked with us individually on the wards, which served to develop deeper relationships. Penny experienced God in amazing ways and fostered in me a desire to know Him in a much less rigid, rules-governed way than I had at this time begun to develop.

26

The beginning of "rules to relationship"

Penny was a brilliant nurse, but also a vibrant and bouncy person, loved by everybody on the wards. One cost of being a Christian was a challenge to attend a weekly Bible study with a Christian group. This meant I had to request to be off duty on Wednesday evenings when I was on ward work. The group was well known throughout the hospital. Some wards loved the ways members worked, but others resented the number of staff asking to be off duty on a Wednesday. We were encouraged to be polite and flexible but honest with our reasons for our request. I found this difficult but learned to ask for God's help and He was always faithful. On several wards a Christian member of staff would grant me favour and also look out for me in my work and training. On one or two wards I was ostracised for my faith, but often a Christian patient or older member of staff would keep me encouraged, and Penny also helped me through on these difficult wards.

I felt well supported over the normal ups and downs of these years of my nurses' training, and had the joy of seeing several colleagues come to know Jesus. My days off, especially after night duty, added together to make almost a full week. I popped home on the train and enrolled with a great riding school where I was invited to join the student instructors' classes. I learned so much and loved the honour of being invited and the challenge of the lessons. The horses were lovely and as instructor students we were responsible for all the horse care and management.

But towards the end of my second year of nurse training, my body began to show signs of wear and tear from my childhood experiences. No one could understand the cause of my increasing ill health, and I couldn't tell anyone.

OK, so it wasn't all plain sailing in my nursing years. I'm conscious I need to be real and honest. It really helped me, yesterday, to realise what good support I had in these two nursing years. Sometimes we fail to see the miraculous wisdom of God's church and ministry through His believers. Caught up in my own private, messed-up world, I could never have survived those university and nursing days. I would either have gone back into the bondage I first knew or, if I could have plucked up the courage, I knew moments when suicide seemed an option.

Onlookers often scorn suicide, but there are points in deep emotional pain when life is just too hard to contemplate. There's even a stage called "beyond suicide", where people don't even have the energy to end their pain. Another disastrous way of escape is mental psychosis or multiple personality – now known as disassociation. I've nursed, experienced, and counselled people in all these situations. Mental and emotional illness is very real. The more I see of it, the more I grieve that we are so quick to judge those who've lost control of their heart and mind. They need as much care and patience as people with physical illness. They also need as much dignity and respect as we can offer within God's boundaries. The mentally ill can make demands on family and the medical professions, social services, and churches that drain those individuals who show concern. The drain is rooted in the sick person's loss of their core self, which renders them unable to take personal responsibility. They are often full of shame and remorse for how they are, but any suggestion of this can cause angry or desperate and manipulative outbursts.

We often teach church prayer teams how to recognise and manage these needy individuals. The experience of having been one and ministered to many has given me insight from both sides, and I know that God is so clever and so gracious.

> *If you want to read further, I recommend "Stop Walking On Egg Shells" by Mason and Kreger, and "Boundaries" by Cloud and Townsend.*

In brief, witnessing human nakedness and illness, coupled with high responsibility in work and high expectations in training, I began to struggle emotionally. I was also increasingly challenged by the nurses' Christian group as time went on. I was invited into special leadership training with demanding requirements in Bible study, ministry, and leadership, and several meetings – some of which were late at night after an evening shift, or as early as 5 a.m. before a morning shift.

I was still driven to please anyone in authority so I pushed myself close to exhaustion trying to be a witness for God by reaching excellence in commitment to the group and also in my ward work and the extra study required of the six pioneer students. My five colleagues simply did their hospital work and study and had some fun in their lives. I, however, believed that God required more of me if He had honoured me with leadership training.

As my health began to fail, my tutors suggested I move back into the nurses' home. It was on-site, whereas the lovely flat with Fiona and friends involved a forty-five-minute journey before and after every shift or meeting. My move out of the flat was helped by a three-month diversion in our nurse training. The six of us spent this time together in a nurses' home in a coastal city where we worked in a psychiatric hospital and received special teaching and training.

27

Descent into depression

> *I'm beginning to struggle again because I'm touching on the start of my descent into depression.*

I think my slide into breakdown began on night duty during my paediatric training. I loved the ward I was on, and the staff, the children, and the Thames view were delightful. One night, however, I began to feel low and unwell, and had somehow got a rose thorn embedded in my finger. My seniors noticed my hand swelling and a red line which appeared as the night wore on. I was instructed to rest my hand and arm even though I was on duty. As soon as morning staff were due, I was sent to a nurses' clinic where I was quickly seen, carefully examined, and given strong medication and instructions to rest for two weeks. I was overwhelmed by the respect and care I was being given; it was a completely new experience.

The doctor who had seen my swollen hand (and arm by now) called me back in to see him and a nursing sister. They expressed grave concern that I had left the thorn in for several days and seemed to find it very hard to understand how I could manage to think I was fit for work. Their comments and questions began to come too close to some of my childhood experiences, so I quickly closed down. I suspect they made notes in my file.

I could have been lonely for my two weeks' sick leave but Fiona and other nurse colleagues were extremely kind and cared for me. Programmed as I was, however, I began to feel guilty and to listen to accusations in my mind that I was sly and manipulative, weak and not fit to be alive. I daren't share my negative thoughts with my positive friends. I simply became sad and tearful. They noticed and encouraged me to hang on to God, His love, and His Word.

I was relieved to return to work, and soon moved to a surgical ward where we cared for patients with severe cancer, or heart and kidney transplants. It was a challenge for me to encounter terminal illness and family loss and grief. I was still unable to come to terms with losing Grandpa, my friend and my mother's mother. My night terrors and mental torment increased and I began to feel exhausted. From my training in mental health I could see I was probably quite depressed and my anxiety was manifesting somatically.

I began to suffer body memories which included knee and shoulder pain and, later, severe internal pain and even haemorrhage from old childhood wounds. Sadly and embarrassingly, these were in sexual areas and other private parts of me so I didn't want anyone to know.

By now I had left the flat and returned to the nurses' home. My mental health work had been taxing but I had, however, begun to pursue a deeper walk with God through attending a church and house group outside my Christian group and also through prayer and lovely fellowship with Theresa. Another of our six became interested in our faith.

Mental health work and instruction led us all to ask many questions. I took these questions to God and found Him leading me through the Bible to some very helpful answers.

During this time, I was obliged by my father to visit my sister's godfather on all my days off, who acted as my guardian. He was a high-ranking Freemason and my father's best friend, as they had grown up together in the same village. He was now a serving naval officer based near to my university. He and his wife only had one son and it was clear that he and Dad wanted us to marry. Dad was also keen that I would not move too far from my childhood training, and part of my guardian's task was to watch over me and keep me in those ways of thinking during this time away from my dad. My guardian's opposition to my faith was a significant factor in my attending a church outside my Christian group. He and his wife were scornful of and strongly opposed to my faith. They took me to many Masonic events for ladies and encouraged me to move in naval and Masonic circles. I became aware of increased spiritual disturbance when I was with this family and at Masonic events. The naval base, however, had some special riding stables with high-grade horses, and an instructor who was an ex-jockey.

I couldn't resist weekends at the naval base followed by a ride. I soon took up private jumping lessons with the jockey and passed exams set by naval stables staff. This meant I could ride better and better horses and even ride out alone.

I was sliding into trouble.

28

Crisis and comfort

Mercifully, at this vulnerable time, the university branch of my lovely Christian group didn't forget me. I think the London nurses' branch got in touch with them and they were all concerned about me. I spent an afternoon near the university with Maddy, the charge nurse who had been my first Christian contact in London. She bought me ice cream then and she did it again now, and I was deeply impacted by the love I received that afternoon. In the midst of that, however, I was challenged about my Masonic activities and my sense of having to spend so much time with my father's friend. I was even asked if there was anything going on between me and the son of that family. I heard my first teaching about not dating a non-Christian. Little did those wonderful people know that the thought of marriage and dating held huge fear and revulsion for me.

I was glad, however, that they had challenged and taught me. Not long before I was due to return to London, this son expressed his "love" for me and his sense that we should marry. His arguments were all around the need to continue family ties and traditions. I was glad to be able to say no, and amazed how courageously I was able to profess my faith in God and my desire to marry a person of His choosing, or to remain single. The son urged at length, but God gave me the courage to stand firm. Dad and his friend were clearly angry and displeased, and I never felt at ease with them after making my stand. Their favour toward me had definitely drained away. To add insult to injury, I also felt I should refuse all invitations to Masonic events, although I had no idea why. My friends had been very clear on this, and I followed my sense of right before God. I am now much more informed and glad He rescued me in those early days of ignorance.

Once back at the hospital my somatic problems increased. They seemed to get worse after I'd made my stand against Freemasonry and the family's ideas of an arranged marriage for me. I had to visit numerous specialists in the hospital where I was a trainee. I was examined over and over again and felt ashamed, dirty, and embarrassed. The night terrors were getting worse and I was fighting tormenting lies and accusations all day.

In addition, I was working on a ward where the sister was not a Christian and was angered by requests from nurses who wanted to attend the Wednesday evening Bible study or an occasional Sunday service.

With all my torment and physical issues, my work was suffering. The ward sister was often frustrated with me, especially for being slow. I was slow because I was terrified of making mistakes as a result of my tormented mind as well as my weary, painful body. Eventually I began to make mistakes as well as being slow.

I left that ward and began work on a gynaecological unit. In my days of sport when I had sustained some knee damage, my father had used the excuse of treating my knee to enter the bathroom while I was bathing. I began now to develop knee pain and swelling during my ward work. My previous ward was at the far end of the hospital, so bloods and other specimens were a long walk from the laboratories. I was often asked to take specimens there. One day my knee locked completely. I was terrified. Somehow (I now know it was because of associated memories) my knee trouble filled me with guilt and shame. The locked knee was excruciating, but I forced myself to walk back to the ward. The ward sister was again angry with me and sent me straight to casualty. I was still in uniform, so the casualty sister hastily pushed me into a side room, saying, "It is improper for nurses in uniform to be seen amongst patients." I was confused and even more embarrassed.

The other staff and the specialist were, however, delightful. I was given painkillers and a bed and later taken straight to theatre. This was the only way my knee could be unlocked.

Fiona still lived in the beautiful London flat. In all my pain and confusion, I had begun to withdraw from the Christian group. I was living in the nurses' home where I knew nobody and this saved me embarrassment. After the surgery to unlock my knee, hospital staff were concerned to get me home and somebody contacted my first ward sister. She was a lovely, lively Christian lady who knew Fiona and contacted her. At least, I think that's what happened; I was too woozy to be clear on anything.

I lived on the third floor of the nurses' home, which concerned the ward sister and my friends. The ward sister herself organised meals for me for a day or two. One day she carried a meal to me all the way from her ward. I was overwhelmed by such kindness but my guilt and shame and torment were increasing.

Fiona and this sister approached a senior nurse who lived in the same nurses' home as me. She came to visit and try to find out why I seemed so low and troubled. As I recovered health, I told her more about my stress and even shared about some of my bodily ailments. She pushed me to return to the nurses' clinic even though she was aware I was reluctant to feel even more shame.

With rest and physiotherapy, I was able to return to work. As the gynae ward had lighter duties at night, I was put on duty there until the date for further knee surgery. I had two months of medical ward experience to complete before my exams for state registration.

The plan was for me to do two or three weeks of night duty before surgery. After surgery I would need two months' rest and physio-therapy. No one could care for me in London so I had to go back home. My parents, concerned by what they saw as my foolish decisions regarding Freemasonry and marriage, were glad to be able to spend this time with me. They wanted me well away from Christian fanatics. A long visit home was anticipated, but first of all I had to face surgery.

By now I was suffering considerable anxiety. I managed a few days on the gynae ward and two or three nights. The staff and patients were lovely and the pace was much slower than on the surgical ward. One early morning, however, everything changed. At the end of the night shift our job was to switch the oven on to heat it up for the cook to prepare breakfast. I went into the kitchen to prepare the oven and found the top gas lights lit. This was, I think, to warm up the kitchen but I'll never really know why they were left on with four sets of naked flames burning.

It seems that someone may have thought they'd lit the oven. In my tiredness and distress, I had started making mistakes. I was close by the kitchen and smelled gas. Ignoring the naked flames on top, I went in to investigate. I opened the oven door and the next thing I was aware of was an orderly screaming as I was enveloped in flames.

I must have put my hands over my eyes. The oven door opened downwards, and, as I had only opened it a little before the explosion, it must have closed again and protected my body. I think my stiff starched nurses' apron probably also acted as a fire shield.

Fortunately, someone had the presence of mind to switch off the gas. Several others ran to the kitchen and screamed at the sight of me. The ward sister came from somewhere and opened up a cool room with a long sofa in it. That's where I came back to consciousness as a kind lady doctor woke me up to tell me I had second-degree burns. My eyes were hard to open but I could see blurred images through the small slits I managed to force apart despite considerable swelling. My hands and arms had taken most of the brunt of the flames.

As we were in an outlying hospital there was discussion about getting me to the main hospital as soon as possible. An ambulance could have been summoned, but the doctor had already examined me and was confident there were no third-degree burns, so deep infection was unlikely. The laundry man was present on the ward and I was asked how I felt about travelling with him in his van rather than waiting for an ambulance.

I must have agreed, so the laundry man delivered me to the walk-in casualty department. The sister was not happy with this arrangement and put me in a wheelchair straightaway. I began to feel very low, stupid, and guilty. Everyone was extremely kind and concerned, but I had already been in a heightened state of sensitivity before the accident. I remember vague worries about blindness and a scarred face, which was the possibility I heard the doctors discussing. My struggle was against terrible torment. Somehow, all I could hear were demonic voices from the past laughing and mocking and threatening. This, it seemed, was retribution for seeking to stand against all I'd been taught and trained and groomed for in my early childhood. They were going to force me back, or destroy me and my loved ones. Little wonder then, that when my good friend Maddy was killed in a car accident shortly after this, I felt terrified and responsible.

Eventually I left hospital and found myself back in the nurses' home. I remember very little except lying alone in bed and suffering deep, persistent torment. I know Fiona and other friends visited, but I felt distant from them. I was in shock and too low to engage with anyone.

Over several weeks my skin recovered and re-grew, but it was all a horrible blur. I think I remained in the nurses' home right up to my admission for knee surgery.

By the grace of God, Fiona was working on the orthopaedic ward. The ward sister there and her charge nurse were also lovely Christian women, and Penny had good reason to visit the ward too because Fiona was a graduate nursing student. For some reason, I was admitted several days before my operation. This may have been general practice, but I've a feeling strings were pulled because senior staff were concerned about me.

Penny was experiencing God in amazing ways. She was particularly vivacious and full of life, and her new-found faith filled her and everyone she met with infectious joy. She arrived on the ward soon after my admission. She and Fiona both expressed thanks to God that we could all be in this together. I felt desperately alone and near to tears. Being in their presence was, somehow, physically painful and the tormenting voices were very loud.

Fiona had to work but Penny was able to stay with me. She tried to make conversation but I was incapable. I think staff put my low mood and silence down to the trauma of the explosion. Everyone was concerned, and Penny visited daily. She had a deep grasp of Scripture and all it said about God's power and love. She gave me individual verses to ponder, because she perceived I couldn't focus on the written Word. This was put down to my stress and swollen eyes, but I knew it was also the pain and internal noise I experienced when I tried to have anything to do with God.

Eventually, Penny suggested I get out of bed. She proceeded to encourage me to change my sheets and tidy my locker. The physical activity was therapeutic. Penny saw this and came daily to do active tasks with me. As I relaxed and gained confidence that my body was recovering and had growing strength, I was able to hear and digest more of her words. God's peace began to return to me, especially when she visited. Fiona and the ward sister were kind. Other visitors were limited because it was clear I needed peace and rest.

By the time I was ready to go to theatre I must have appeared quite normal. As the operation approached, however, I was paralysed with fear. Tormenting voices were telling me I would die, and I was haunted by memories of being sedated, abused, and tortured as a child. I really believed I was going to die under anaesthetic.

Penny came on the day of surgery. She spent the whole morning keeping me active and praying for me. She ordered special medication from the ward doctors who trusted her wisdom. Fiona was allowed to take me down to the anaesthetic room where I somehow went to sleep, but woke to cruel torment. Everyone was baffled by my adverse reactions, which they attributed to the trauma of the explosion.

Three tough weeks later I was put on the train home, where I spent two very lonely months. My mother was descending into depression; my father was facing staff strikes and my sister was abroad and a major worry to the family.

I returned to London in August. Penny offered me private tuition for my nursing exams, and I met with her regularly and blossomed under her love and care. Learning anatomy, physiology, and nursing care in her fun ways was a great distraction from the tormenting voices and miserable memories. I buried myself in study.

Penny also enlisted Fiona. Together they helped me to talk about my fears for my family and to pray with them to put my family into God's care. That helped me considerably. My eyes were fully recovered so I now had no excuse not to read my Bible. Penny and Fiona helped me push through what they saw as demonic opposition to my reading. None of us realised the depth of my bondage, but God lovingly covered that until years later in my life. For now, simply declaring Jesus as Lord until my body stopped shaking was bringing me greater peace and much less resistance. The voices ceased as I pushed through with prayer or by quoting Scripture. Penny taught me to refuse all condemning or accusing thoughts and helped me to seek to enjoy freedom in God's love.

I passed my exams with flying colours. All my colleagues had gone home for the summer, but I had to do two months' work on the medical ward. I don't know if Penny arranged it, but the sister of that ward was a committed Christian. She encouraged me in everything I did. I was a senior nurse by now and needed encouragement to face increased responsibility. The love I received during my long stay on the orthopaedic ward had also taught me about what helps a patient to feel safe and well cared-for. Penny helped me to use this knowledge, and fear left me. I genuinely enjoyed giving the same love and care to patients that I had received. Penny, Fiona, and my other Christian friends in London positively supported me during these two months.

I blossomed.

The day to leave my beloved ward came all too quickly. The ward sister begged me to stay in nursing and offered me a senior position on her ward. I was tempted, but firmly believed God wanted me to complete the whole course, which required that the degree and health visiting components be completed at university. So I returned to the south.

I had developed a desire to bless others and to share my faith, so much so that I chose to accept a place in a hall of residence. I wanted to mix with all kinds of students, and certainly didn't want to be exiled in lodgings as I had been in my first year.

The first term was fun. I made friends with Alice, a psychology student. She was a gentle Christian girl whose mother had died when she was quite young, and she cared deeply for her widowed father. I loved her care for her father but felt a growing guilt struggling to love my father in the same way. My fear of my parents dying without Jesus began to haunt me again. Alice's mother had died, so I knew parents could die early.

My fears increased, as did my old torment and flashbacks to horrendous memories. All of this – added to my difficult mental hospital nursing experience – began to increase my stress. I fought it by increasing my hours in prayer and evangelism.

During the second term both my parents became seriously depressed. Dad was drinking heavily, especially at Masonic events. Mum was worried about him, and fearful. My sister was back in England, living nearby but also suffering with depression.

I rang home weekly because my mother "needed it". She would write me letters telling me how cruel I was to have left home, and that I was to blame for the family's struggles. I believed her. Now that she had begun to live upstairs in the house and Dad downstairs, they wanted separate phone calls from me. They said they needed my support and it was my duty as a daughter. My sister also wanted contact. This was well before the days of mobile phones, and each call involved queuing to use the public phone in the hall of residence.

In addition, I began to envy students with happy homes. I became jealous of Alice, because she was loved by everyone, including her father, and had aunts and uncles and godparents who pampered her. She took me home with her, but somehow that made my jealousy worse. I felt evil; she was so loving and I wasn't.

My work began to fail and I felt a failure as a daughter. As accusations and torment grew, I tried to combat them as Penny and Fiona had taught me. Soon all my time after lectures was spent in hours of prayer. When I couldn't sleep I got up to pray and fight to read my Bible. When I could sleep I set an alarm to be sure I'd be up to pray at 6 a.m. or earlier. I was trying to pummel my body and sacrifice myself but somehow I only felt farther and farther away from God's love and favour.

29

Learning He is always enough

My writing went well yesterday, but I felt myself falling into the feelings of that awful fourth year at university. Part of me wants to leave it behind and part of me wants to keep writing as expression can be therapeutic. Expression can also, however, simply lead back into old feelings. Somehow, I need to make sure I bring these feelings to God at some point and hear and receive His comfort and healing. As I said before, I've never really processed these difficult years after I left home and my occult training. I'm scared of opening up a whole new can of worms. I'm scared, too, that I won't be able to function if I do open the can.

This is a fear that clients often meet with when they consider therapy or prayer ministry. As prayer ministers, we need to be careful how we use words of knowledge. I used to think everything I was given in discernment needed to be shared straightaway. I've now learned that there is great wisdom in being more cautious and humble. Receiving revelation about someone or something is a gift from God for me or someone else, and I need to stay humble. Realising this is a gift to help me show God's love to another, I find it wise to ask God what He wants me to do with what He's revealed. Sometimes He says, "Share it." Sometimes He says, "Hold it," or simply, "Pray." It can be dangerous or premature to blurt out what He gives every time He gives something.

I think I'll roll on with the facts of what happened, rather than trying to analyse. These chapters are designed to be the link to my writing about my depressions and I need to realise I'm not yet in a place to teach from them. I want to point out God's wonderful care but, in all honesty, I think I fell into severe depression because He seemed so distant in those times.

A symptom of depression is utter hopelessness. For the first time in my life, that's where I was heading. For all my attempts at extra prayer and Bible reading, I was finding no solace and felt no help in God. I confess that I didn't realise I could ask Him for help. I felt bad, evil, and unlovable.

In London, I had learned that prayer, service, and God's Word were powerful. I had all the love and close support of Penny and Fiona and the happy medical ward; I felt good and therefore close to God. When my occult training pressed in, I was able to stand against it. I was using distraction through work or God's Word, and because I was working so hard, family contact diminished.

At university, however, my weekends and evenings were deemed available time in my family's estimation, so they demanded much more attention. As their depressions increased, I felt more and more guilty and responsible. I think the crunch came when my parents told me that my sister was suicidal. She was suffering such severe depression that from time to time her limbs would paralyse. I felt I needed to go home, but my university schedule was intense.

Most students, including Alice, had one degree to complete, which involved two to eleven hours' lecture time each week, plus additional reading and essay writing. Dissertations were also underway. My course, in contrast, had twenty-three hours of lecture time plus health visiting practice and essays. My lovely Christian colleague had decided to pursue a career in nursing in the London hospital and I missed her.

The colleague who had considered Christianity during our mental health training had her own issues in this fourth year. Her father suffered a stroke, an event which increased my fears for my own family. She didn't complete the course, leaving only four of the original six of us.

Alice's presence also began to haunt me. She talked often about the death of her mother. She was studying psychology so, for her, grief was an issue to be explored. It fascinated her but it terrified me. My psychology training was different as it was tailored to our Administrative degree and our Health Visiting Certificate. I longed for room to explore like Alice. I grew increasingly envious of her freedom and academic support. I also envied all students doing a straight degree, and there were a lot of them to be jealous of.

I think my final collapse came when the father of another colleague had a heart attack and died during our second term. Melanie tried to continue the course, but eventually went home to be with her mother. She was my only colleague in hall and I suddenly felt very alone. The remaining two students found the fourth year impossible. One dropped the degree and another dropped the Health Visiting Certificate. Suddenly I was the only original left and the only student with such a ridiculous schedule. I felt responsible for my family, but I felt God had given me a place on the course so I needed to complete it. I also began to feel that God was angry about my selfishness and jealousy; I was ceasing to be truly loving to my family, my colleagues, my Christian group, and "the lost". I pushed deeper into sacrificing myself, with more prayer, more Bible study, more family support, more evangelism. I hated myself. I couldn't even do these things well and my university work was suffering. My brain seemed scrambled; I couldn't focus.

I left the big student church and started to creep into a quieter Anglican church. During one evening service fear overwhelmed me. I began to tremble as visions of my family flashed before me. I heard the word "suicide" screaming at me over and over again. I felt God was angry with me, accusing me of not supporting my sister and parents, yet part of me knew He wanted me to be at university. All I remember is that the confusion and shaking increased until I was faced with the blackness and terror I'd met as a child in night rituals. These had never before manifested in a public place. I tried to escape but people had seen my trauma. They came to calm me down. Now I was beyond terrified – I began to scream and finally collapsed on the floor. I daren't tell anyone what was going on. I've no idea how I got back to my halls of residence, and just have blurred memories of a chair and a cup of tea and kind people.

I knew what I'd encountered must never be spoken about. I remained in bed for several days. On the Wednesday or Thursday, a kind Christian hall mate visited, bringing me a cup of tea and asking if he could stay and chat. I told him I couldn't speak to him. I was extremely scared because he was male and – to be honest – I think I really liked him. I certainly couldn't process that sort of thinking, but he persisted. What surprised me was that there was nothing sexual in his approach. He sat at a good distance and simply encouraged me to talk about my course and interests as I drank my mug of tea. He then encouraged me to talk to my Christian group, of which he was a member, and arranged a chat for me with my friend and mentor, Georgia, and another older girl.

I was scared to say anything about that embarrassing Sunday, but I discovered that Georgia attended that church. She encouraged me to see a university doctor who prescribed antidepressants and suggested I go home to my family as I was so concerned about them. My tutors agreed and I returned home to work through my first depression, which I've described in Chapter 21. I'm not sure the roots of my breakdown were touched during that time, but God came close again and did everything I needed at that stage.

> *The deepest root causes of my depressions and anxieties were not revealed and healed until I was in my fifties. As I have mentioned, in Matthew 13 God teaches about the wheat and the tares being allowed to grow together, and that was certainly happening here for me. I'm sure Georgia and the others knew there was serious demonic interference in my condition. Praise God, she had the wisdom not to try to plunge into deliverance. My emotional damage was far too serious. I did not have the core strength or faith in God to stand either therapy or deep ministry. We need to be very humble and careful how we help people with complex troubles like mine.*

30

Final return to the south

My time at home, aged twenty-two, was spent pouring my heart out to God. Georgia and my male fellow student gave me permission to be real with Him. My GP at home relieved me of my sense of responsibility for my family. He began to take note of the condition they were in and offered help, which my mother accepted. I spent many hours walking and talking with my father, but I don't know if he ever went for medical help at this stage. My sister made plans to move back home having secured a job close by. She was to start in the September, by which time I was back at university.

During my time at home I met with the curate at my old family church. Georgia and I chatted on the phone each week and I could call whenever I needed. My helpers encouraged me to be real with God and to soak up His love. I was amazed how faithfully He began to speak lovingly into my stresses and distresses. At that stage that was all I needed or could tolerate. I read a lot of Amy Carmichael's writing[29], learning how she suffered long-term illness and found God in the darkest places.

The days at home were quiet and lonely. My parents knew I was very unwell so they seemed to take the pressure off me. I think they hoped I'd return home, give up my faith, and return to what they called "how it used to be". I'm not sure what they thought that meant.

---

[29] e.g. *Candles in the Dark;* Christian Literature Crusade (1982); ISBN 9780875080857; and *Rose from Brier;* Christian Literature Crusade (1972); ISBN 9780875080772.

God, however, was calling me back to university, to greater independence from my family and to greater dependence on Him. Georgia, the GP, and the curate helped me see that I wouldn't kill my family by beginning to live my own life. Georgia and the curate were emphatic that obeying God's call in my life was the best thing I could do for myself, and for everyone else. I began to believe them and to hear God's voice again. He was, undoubtedly, calling me back to the south. In response, I listed twenty-five reasons why I couldn't do this. He then showed me Isaiah 45 which says that He can level mountains and cut through iron and bronze obstacles. So I gave Him my twenty-five "mountains" and went back to university by pure faith. He levelled every single one.

My tutors set several rules about my return to university, and my parents were heavily involved in the discussion. They all blamed the Christian group for my breakdown, and I was told I should not attend any Christian group meetings or take part in Bible study of any sort, but they couldn't have been further from the truth. I was treated as if I had minor significance in the decisions that were made. Georgia and the curate, however, helped me to maintain a level of freedom and adult autonomy. After all, I was twenty-two years old and a qualified nurse who could take responsibility for a full ward of patients. I had been seriously ill, though, and I carried the fear of the blackness and screaming experience I'd had in the church. That still frightened me, and I couldn't tell anyone.

I was asked to live with Beatrice, a retired tutor, rather than in a hall of residence. I accepted, and this reduced my contact with Alice and other regular degree students. That eased my attacks of envy, so I felt better. My lectures were with large numbers of students I didn't know, or with those simply doing the health visiting course after nursing. I could study in relative isolation, and this suited me.

I didn't attend group meetings or Bible study but I did meet weekly with Georgia for a coffee. What was "coffee" to my tutors was invaluable time when Georgia nurtured my walk with God. Through the week I would ask God for one verse of Scripture each day which I'd learn and carry through the day, letting God speak through it. Initially, I did this for only five minutes, but this grew into a constant dialogue with my loving Heavenly Father. I was able to share and test all God was saying each week with Georgia.

After each phone call home, Beatrice, who used to be a social work tutor, was a real help to me, enabling me to understand my parents' pain, but also showing where I needed to curb my sense of responsibility. Unfortunately, however, after meeting my parents she began to relate to them independently from me. She invited them to come and stay at her house. Sadly, after that first visit, she gave them an invitation to come whenever they liked. I felt betrayed and vulnerable, and I didn't understand why.

I survived two terms and then the Easter vacation arrived. I had been loving the studying we were doing, especially psychology. I was also enjoying my health visiting placement. My fieldwork instructor was a widowed pastor's wife. She and her husband had worked abroad in some difficult places and she had questioned her faith a lot, probably due to her bereavement when, at an early age, she had been left with three young children. She treated me like an older daughter and sometimes I felt almost like her confidante. Best of all was her sense of humour. She laughed most at herself, which freed me to be myself and to make mistakes. I flourished in this environment – so much so that the Christian group spotted me as a potential leader and I was invited to attend a leaders' conference during the five-week Easter break. My parents planned to visit, stay with Beatrice for a few days, and then take me home from university. The conference was to be held during those few days of their planned stay. Three of the days were clear but on the fourth day I would need to leave for the conference hall at about 5 p.m. My trunk still needed to be taken home, so I thought my parents might visit and drive home, or stay longer with Beatrice and then spend the long Easter with me when I was taken home by friends from the conference.

But my father took offence. He refused to visit at all if I was going to leave early – although in reality it was only by half a day. I tried to explain that this conference was an opportunity I didn't want to miss. I was not planning on any form of leadership training or responsibility until the following year. My mother seemed to understand, but Dad continued to be furious. He had several weeks' notice of the potential change of plans and chose to cut off all contact in those weeks, calling me a disgrace as a daughter. My mother relayed his messages and then, for two weeks, there was complete silence. I had insisted on going to the conference, making my own plans for my luggage to go home ahead of me and for my journey home. Mum said she thought Dad would still let me go home for the vacation. He, however, refused to speak to me in person. I was sad they wouldn't visit, but made plans for the three or four days between the end of term and the conference.

Imagine my surprise when my parents arrived on my doorstep! I had a conflicting mixture of feelings. Part of me was pleased I hadn't been thrown out of home again, and part of me was worried I'd have to change all my plans, some of which were preparation for the conference. My Christian friends encouraged me to spend time with my parents. They also invited them to a meal at their home. I was still assured of a place at the conference.

My parents' stay was hard. Dad was surly. He and Mum loved Beatrice and her dog, Hugo, but were angry and derogatory when alone with me, and even with my friends. When I asked Dad what had changed his mind about the visit his comment alarmed me: "Never let it be said that I refused to visit you." I was troubled. He had clearly refused, but now I seemed to be to blame. He also grumbled about the journey, the shortness of his stay, and the influence of my friends on me. He hated the Christian group. At the time, I couldn't understand why, but now I see how two spiritual kingdoms were clashing. My mother was miserable because Dad was miserable. Again, I seemed to be to blame. Beatrice saw none of this and enthused about how gracious and amenable my parents were. Now even Beatrice was suggesting that any relational issues must stem from my own flawed thinking.

I began to doubt my own mind. With Dad in the house, I panicked at night. I wanted to lock my bedroom door but I couldn't. I felt evil, but would still push a chair against the door. One night someone tried to come in and couldn't. I heard Dad swearing on the landing but he didn't force the door open. I'm not sure the chair would have moved that far as I'd wedged it well.

I was sad, losing confidence, and very troubled, and the shaking began to return. Mum and Dad looked bereft when I left for the conference. They were staying with Beatrice for another night, and I felt appalling. By the time we arrived at the conference, I was struggling to hold back tears. I couldn't explain why – I wasn't even sure myself. People were very kind to me. Georgia was a senior leader and speaker so she was busy all weekend but introduced me to some lovely people. The teaching was wonderful. The songs were heartening, especially one with words something like, "My Lord knows the way through the wilderness, all I have to do is follow." I felt I was in a real wilderness.

One day there was a most significant moment. The national ministry leader, whom I'd met in London, recognised me in the ladies' cloakroom and asked me how I was. I told her a little about my family's trials, and nearly cried at her most beautiful look of compassion. I fled into the nearest cubicle but when I came out she was still there. At the door of the cloakroom she took my hand and said, "You're going to be OK." For some reason that filled me with strength, like a surge of God's love. On the strength of that moment and my conference notes, I managed to navigate my way through the holiday at home.

On my return, finals were looming. I planned to study for ten hours a day. As I couldn't settle in the stress of the library I worked in my lodgings. I couldn't work out why, but I now felt vulnerable in my bedroom, and kept a chair at my door. Beatrice tried to come into my room one day and was worried to see that I'd put a chair at the door, but she accepted my weird excuse about needing the chair space when I was studying. It was untrue. All I knew was that the memory of Dad arriving unannounced and sleeping in this house had really unsettled me. My mind kept wandering to unpleasant memories at night and flashbacks broke into my days.

I began to find focusing hard in the day and I couldn't sleep at night. I tried an evening service at my church but was terrified of another black, screaming attack. I found it best to arrive after the worship and to leave before the last hymn or prayers. That way no one could speak to me, but the teaching was my lifeline for the week. Georgia was often away on speaking engagements, but during one of our coffees she encouraged me to see my university GP. He assumed I was experiencing normal student finals stress and gave me stronger medication which helped me sleep at night. This aided my focus and I began to reach a more even keel. The doctor saw me every two or three weeks. I managed five hours' work a day, but it was effective. I was enjoying the study and my favourite subject was still psychology.

One rainy day during this time, I met a Japanese student at the bus stop. I felt God prompt me to go and talk to her, so I did. I don't know what happened to the bus, but it didn't come for ages. I'd learned to be real about my simple faith. Okimo, my new friend, was excited. She said she'd just begun to think about God and invited me to her lodgings for a meal. As we chatted more, I shared the gospel, using an analogy of getting on the train of faith, not simply saying you believe it takes a particular route but committing to the journey. Okimo met with me weekly. One Saturday she went to a country market where she was miraculously given a Japanese CD by a stall-keeper. It used the exact same analogy about the train, only instead of, "I believe this train goes to Edinburgh, London, or wherever," the speaker said, "I believe the train goes to Tokyo." Okimo told me she was so amazed she wanted to get on the train to heaven that Jesus offered and commit her life to Him. I prayed with her as she gave her life to Christ, and she never looked back.

I also made a friend in the university riding club. She was a social work student who owned two horses at her home in the north. We rode and chatted a lot and she too came to faith. Several other people got to know me and enjoyed my deep, simple faith. Fruit was springing up all around me. I felt approved by God – life was going well.

Unfortunately, around this time, my landlady Beatrice invited a group of friends over. They seemed pleasant, but one of them decided to play a recording of a spiritualist talking to the spirit of a dead person. I was very disturbed by it, and the blackness and shaking returned. She questioned and challenged what she called my rigid faith and Beatrice seemed to support her. I began to struggle again.

My fieldwork instructor spotted my growing distress. One day we had a long talk in the car during which I told her about the Easter conference and my parents, although I didn't tell her about Dad and my bedroom. She felt I was suffering from stress and phoned my tutors. She saw my potential but also my distress. She and Beatrice helped me entrust it to God until after my exams, which she and my GP arranged for me to sit in the medical centre. There I could be cared for and kept quiet and unstressed. Their support and wisdom helped me. My GP saw me weekly and Georgia encouraged me to work all I could and to give the rest to God. My dad even sent a letter about Jesus telling the disciples to put their nets out again on the right side of the boat after a night when they had caught nothing. I was blessed and amazed by this letter and felt bad for judging him. I wrote to him about my stress and medication and asked him to manage without visits or calls for a while because I wanted to focus on my study; I thought he'd understand. He had suggested at the end of his letter that he could come and stay if I wanted support, which is exactly why I asked him not to visit. I knew having him around would be most unhelpful.

He and Mum did cut contact, as I had requested; my studies were going just well enough; and then the bomb fell. Dad and Mum had made an executive decision. Having chatted with Beatrice, unbeknown to me, they decided to come and stay throughout the weeks before my exams. I was horrified and furious when they arrived on the doorstep.

Dad wanted to rearrange and oversee my study programme. Mum wanted attention and company in my relaxation time. I was beside myself with anxiety and started to have serious blackouts. I went to see my GP and met Georgia in a temporary escape from my parents. I felt so ungrateful to them, but I wasn't sure I was wrong in my sense of injustice. I had been so clear with them.

Georgia, my GP, and my fieldwork tutor encouraged me to insist on my own plans for revision. I carved out five to seven hours a day for study. I chatted with Beatrice and my parents together and they agreed to five hours, but no more. I was angry and panicking. Deep down, however, I knew I could only really manage one or two hours of study now. So I settled for having five hours alone in my bedroom each day, putting the chair firmly over the door. The GP had said I could double my medication at night. By doing that, I managed to sleep. Beatrice entertained my parents, which was such a blessing. She also fed me well, morning, noon and night, and I went to bed very early.

I spent much of my five hours alone in prayer, expressing my anger and fears to God. I felt bad, but knew I could receive His forgiveness for my anger. I entrusted my exams to Him. Towards the end of the revision period I asked God to show me exactly what to study in my two hours of focused time (I slept or prayed for the other three hours). In each of my five exams I had to answer four questions. For each exam God showed me the exact topics I needed for each paper; I'd even practised some of the questions. In each exam, I found exactly four questions – no more, no less – that I could answer, and I felt God was very close the whole time. My fieldwork instructor and others had sent cards wishing me well which Beatrice must have given to the medical centre. I sat my exams there in a lovely quiet room with the cards set up on my desk, and was plied with tea and coffee and other goodies. I loved those exams and must have done extremely well or I wouldn't have passed my degree at all.

My parents were thrilled with my results. Dad was proud to have been such a "help and support" to me. I felt evil and ungrateful that I had struggled with his presence and sought his forgiveness over the holidays. I'm afraid that opened an unhealthy door in our relationship. Dad became my "soulmate". It all became very unhealthy and I don't want to say any more in detail.

I know Mum and Dad wanted me back up north. Now Grandpa's words came back in force. Deep down I knew I needed distance from Dad and home, although I felt so bad about this. Dad had many Masonic contacts and could have pulled strings to get me a job. He introduced me to his male friends. I didn't enjoy their company, and some made sexual advances. Dad was furious with me when I rejected them and tried to tell him why. He told me I had a warped mind. I'd hoped he would protect me and, at least, be jealous for me.

For a break, Dad, Mum, and I spent four days in Jersey. I asked for a separate room in the hotel, and locked the door and spent a lot of time alone. I set aside two hours each evening to read Isaiah and to seek God. Dad was clearly angry with me, but Mum encouraged him to rest during that time. He seemed breathless and very anxious. One day Mum and I met him for an ice cream after a walk. He had been unable to find us and had become uncontrollably angry; we were both concerned about him.

I insisted on my rests, and God was faithful to speak. I read in my Bible, "Depart, depart, go out from there. Touch no unclean thing ... the Lord will go before you."[30] Also, Isaiah 45 brought back all the promises of levelling mountains again. One mountain I had to give to God was my parents' anger and sense of rejection if I were to choose to work in the south. That was my biggest fear. God, however, was being very clear, so on the strength of His Word and an inner assurance I returned south.

I took a nursing post on a paediatric ward and rented a two-bedroom cottage with a Christian who was a secretary at the university. My Christian group began to train me for leadership and I helped lead the nurses' ministry and discipled several young people. I taught groups and was involved in leadership Bible studies, and was asked to return to the big student church.

From November to March that year I struggled along. My father and mother couldn't really come to terms with my decision. They felt bitter and rejected. I felt cruel, but clung to God's Word. Life in the cottage was hard as my housemate was suffering a severe bout of

---

[30] Isaiah 52:11-12 (NIV)

depression. She was lonely because I worked long shifts and she had a nine-to-five job. She also found my inclusion in leadership activities a trial. She felt rejected and second rate, and yet she recognised that her own faith dilemmas prevented her from moving on into any form of leadership. When we were at home together she found conversation difficult. I felt bad, but was being drained by her depressed state. Later, she wisely took hold of her life and applied for a job in Spain. She was a brilliant linguist and that year abroad was the making of her. We went on to share a house with two other professionals and Jeannie was my most faithful friend.

But the years in that small cottage were tough. We were both cold and lonely, and the cottage was very cold and damp. We had wet dew on our bed covers each winter morning. To keep myself afloat I began to work through a study of the whole Bible. I spent my lonely hours feeding on God's Word and answering searching Bible study questions.

I was doing reasonably well until an old childhood injury stopped me in my tracks. Some of the children I was working with were quite hard to lift and my shoulder kept dislocating. I had to visit a hospital doctor who insisted that I needed surgery as I was on my eighth dislocation. Surgery was planned for the end of March.

31

10th March

On 10th March I was on sick leave to let the dislocation heal. It was a horrendous and very strange day, and yet God seemed close in it.

Since our house was so cold and damp I was looking at alternative accommodation. I had been back home in the north for a weekend and on the Monday evening I had a meeting about a potential place in a training house, where I would be living with other professional ladies, one of whom would be the leader responsible for helping us to grow in our discipleship. For some reason – possibly a rail strike – there were no trains that Monday. My father had seemed unwell over the weekend and thought he had a stomach upset. Mum wanted me to stay longer, and said that Dad did too. I was very torn, but prayed and felt I should attend the meeting. I looked for the latest train I could take to get me home. It was actually the only train and was due at 2 a.m. There were no buses so I asked Dad for a lift to the station. Dad was stressed about this and so I suggested a taxi. He said no to a taxi but remained stressed. I felt bad, and when he put me on the train he looked sad and forlorn.

I had my meeting and accepted the place in the flat. I told Jeannie, who was very upset. I spoke to my parents, and they were also upset. I slept badly and woke to the coldest morning ever and to the wettest duvet I'd ever seen.

I cried. I cried out to God. He pointed me to another verse: "I will restore you ... Let this people return to you, but you must not return to them."[31] I was encouraged; God was reassuring me that I was in the right place and I felt He was giving me hope that my family could come back to accepting me, in His timing.

Then I received a phone call and discovered that my life was about to change.

Dad was in intensive care.

He had suffered a heart attack in the early hours of the morning. He was alive, but in danger of an even more major attack.

All I could remember was the troubled face he had had when he put me on the train and the upset about my leaving. I tried to keep out of my mind the refrain he had repeated when I was fourteen and in tears over my beloved, lost Jonty: "You'll be the death of me!" Torment from the rituals pressed in, with angry voices telling me, "This is what happens when you follow 'Grandpa's Jesus'." God seemed distant. I don't know who gave me the phone message about my father or what followed. I only remember the guilt and accusation and darkness pressing in on me.

Somehow, I managed to make it to the home of two new ministry leaders. Georgia was away and I'd been told I was now to relate to my new house leader as Georgia had her own trainees. I found that really hard, and jealousy had crept in again. I'd also been told I was only allowed an hour and a half with my new leader, every two weeks, and we were only to discuss my ministry. This became a real struggle for me later on when I was too ill to minister. I had already been feeling alone and rejected before Dad's heart attack that day, but now all I wanted was to get home to be with him and my poor family. The new ministry leaders hardly knew me, yet they were kind and helpful.

There was now a full-blown rail strike, so a coach was the only option. I left the south at around 10 a.m. and arrived at Dad's hospital after evening visiting time. For some reason, I was wearing my outdoor nurse's uniform and the ward sister realised I understood Dad's dangerous situation. She talked very honestly with me and gave me permission to go and see him. He was now in a private room, doing well but in great danger of a fatal attack in the next forty-eight hours.

God had met me powerfully on the long coach journey. I found Georgia's absence, the new rules around whom I could and couldn't meet, and the lack of time people had for me that day a real trial. I

---

[31] Jeremiah 15:19 (NIV)

couldn't express to any of these relative strangers the guilt and torment I was suffering. I feared they'd judge me as silly or even demented, and I wanted to maintain a reputation as good, mature material for leadership training. I was also embarrassed about my strong, strange ties to my family. My mind was in turmoil.

To focus my thinking, I chose to read the book of Romans from beginning to end on the journey home. If I got through Romans, I decided I would read on until I arrived. Part of me felt I should be open to God giving me someone to share the gospel with as we travelled. I knew I'd be sitting next to someone all the way. I felt pressured, but I had learned from Georgia that God still loved me even when I was weak, ill, or needing to rest, although that wasn't the message I was getting from my new leadership trainer. I decided I hadn't started training yet, so I could be a bit weak with God. I settled for telling Him I would share my faith, but only if He gave me a really good opening in the conversation. God probably agonised over my growing legalism, but He met me just where I was at that time.

I was seated next to a man about my father's age. I took out my smallest Bible and launched into Romans. Periodically I stopped to say sorry to God for so deliberately avoiding this gentleman.

I have a feeling I'd made my way into Corinthians by the time my travelling companion spoke to ask politely what I was reading so avidly. I sensed God's presence as soon as he spoke. I had no problem telling him, "It's the Bible." He was very gracious because that much was blatantly clear. His response was kind: "I know, but can I ask exactly what you're reading in your Bible?" That was such a helpful lead-in for me. I sensed God's presence even more. I told the man the book and the chapter and he seemed overcome with a mixture of joy and excitement, and said, "I'm not a Christian yet but my daughter is. She's been telling me all about Christianity. That's the exact book and chapter she's just shared with me and left me to ponder. How do you understand it?" We talked all the way to the hospital coach stop, and I was able to share the gospel far more clearly than ever before. The man was overjoyed. He wanted to become a Christian, but he wanted to tell his daughter and pray with her so that she could be encouraged.

I felt so blessed by God. That father-daughter relationship gave me hope for my meeting with Dad. I prayed he'd be conscious and that I'd be able to speak with him in a way that would assure him of God's love. I needed God to do that. At this point God's presence was heavily upon me, and I was sure people were praying for me. Georgia had phoned the ministry leaders before I'd left the south. She had told them she wanted me to call her any time I needed, and that message helped me so much. It made me feel less alone and abandoned. There were no mobile phones in those days, so I had no one but God for the ten-hour journey home. I should have been tired, but His presence was upholding me beyond my wildest hopes and expectations. I also felt I could have given life and hope to an unsaved soul on the coach and I knew how blessed his daughter would be. Somehow, I was reassured. For all my failings and torment, God seemed to be willing to come close to me in my time of need. He was even using me to help someone come to faith in Jesus, to have their soul truly saved.

I didn't understand it all, but I did know that God is real. He says we need eternal life and all we have to do is accept Jesus' death for us and invite Him in to forgive our sins and take over our lives. I learned that I could be an instrument for saving life, in His Hands. This went right against all the powerful accusations that tormented me in my darkness and told me I destroyed lives and hope wherever I went unless I bowed to their rules and regulations. I couldn't do that anymore. It seemed wrong before God. For so much of my life I had lived in torment and fear that God might not be able to reach someone as dark and damaged as me. My torment was because I couldn't bring myself to practise my ritual training anymore. I felt trapped in a no man's land if I gave myself any time thinking. At this point, however, there in the hospital, I felt safely held by a love I had only known with Grandpa. I felt held by God. I felt somehow under the shadow of His wing.

Steve's just come home. I left off writing to spend some time with him. I know I've also been taking a break because what I need to write next is so painful. As I have said, much later in life I received ministry for the depths of all the complex experiences I was pushed into as a child. Many a time, even with the strength and maturity I then had in Jesus Christ, I'd reach points where all I could say was, "I can't. I can't. I can't." I was too afraid to encounter the pain and opposition I knew I'd meet when I let the Holy Spirit lead me just far enough into a memory to bring the revelation and healing I needed at that point in time. Little by little, week by week, and now year by year, I have gained confidence that if God is saying, "Do this!" or, "Go there!" then the truth is that I can because He'll go with me and bring me through to healing. So I'm holding on to that confidence now. He would not be asking me to remember and write if His strength were not enough for me. If He asks me to do it then "I can" with His help. So here goes.

The ward sister left me alone with my dad. I knew we only had a few minutes as he was very weak. He needed to be peaceful to avoid another heart attack. I prayed and simply said, "Dad, I'm so sorry this has happened."

His response shook me: "Well, what did you expect, with all that pressure!" He was blaming me and I was speechless. I didn't want an argument as I knew that could kill him, so I prayed silently. A wave of God's love surrounded me and held me, and I felt a deep love and compassion for my dad. For once in my life, his words didn't cut into my heart. Instead, they rolled off. I simply said, "We can look at all that when you're better. But now all you need to know is that God loves you and so do I. I have just travelled straight from the south to be with you. It's taken ten hours, but I'm so glad I'm here. Let me pray for you, then I must go." I prayed for healing, peace, and God's presence to stay with my dad. He seemed to be at peace. He'd gone to sleep; he even seemed to be smiling.

The ward sister met me at the door. She was pleased that he seemed so calm, and said, "I'm sure he's glad you're here." She reiterated the danger he was in for the next forty-eight hours. Although she said nobody could do anything, in that moment I believed God could.

I made my way to Mum's house, where my sister had also now arrived. I phoned Georgia, but Mum didn't like me using her phone. It was also too public for me to say what I wanted, so I made a point of going out to use the public phone box after that first evening.

Mum was stressed when I arrived. She was angry that I lived so far away and insisted I would be no use to anyone if I was going to go south again. I explained that that was where my job was but promised to stay as long as I could. Nothing would appease her so I prayed, and God's love and compassion came again.

Georgia had guessed a call from my parents' house might be too public so she told me to say little. I was also extremely tired and in shock. She wanted to share Romans 5:6 with me, which talks about Christ dying for us while we were still sinners. She wanted me to hold on to that verse, and said that no matter what was said to me, or what I may think I had done wrong, the love of God for me would never change or be weakened. The verse kept me peaceful against all the anger Mum threw at me. I realised she herself was scared, stressed, and traumatised. As she pointed out, she was already suffering from depression and was anxious about who would look after her given that my sister was also depressed. I prayed for strength to weather this storm and managed to get some sleep.

Next morning at breakfast Mum seemed brighter. I became bold again and said, "One thing I really want to do in this situation is to pray. I'd like us to pray together." Mum and Annabella had attended a *Basic Christianity* course, so I felt on safe ground. Mum let me pray; that was as far as it went, but I realised they were both under stress so that was OK.

To bring them the same kind of encouragement I'd received, I tried to share what Georgia had told me about Romans 5. At that point Mum became angry. She said she was a Christian and knew all about praying, but she didn't have to "try to be all romantic about it". I was crushed but felt God's grace to remain calm and loving.

The next forty-eight hours were tough, but Dad did pull through. He was soon on the road to recovery and off the critical list. The ward sister took me aside one day and told me I should consider going back to work. I told her my dilemmas about Mum's and Annabella's depression and how I felt responsible for my family. Her response was amazing; she assured me that good care and family support would be put in place, emphasising that my patients needed me back down south. There was no advantage in my staying with my parents any longer. I only wish she could have helped my family understand, although maybe she did try.

I went back to my job in the south, but without the blessing of my family.

32

My operation

To add to my growing stress, the date came through for my shoulder operation. I could only perform very light duties until I had this surgery, and several nursing colleagues encouraged me not to postpone it. My employers were adamant that I needed to be back to full capacity as soon as possible. My worries about my family seemed to carry no weight in the north or the south, so I accepted the date for surgery.

Because I was nursing staff, I was given a private room, which was possibly a good thing. What was tough, though, was that I had very few visitors. Georgia was away again and Jeannie was still depressed and angry that I planned to leave the cottage. I'd been moved from one job to another after my last shoulder injury, so no one really knew me at work, and all my university friends had by now left the city. My lack of visitors could be easily explained, but it was tough.

Sadly, most of the Christian group were busy with their work and ministry, and I spent long hours alone. It was only two or three weeks since Dad's heart attack. He was out of hospital and doing well, but the family were resentful and didn't seem to grasp that I hadn't much choice. One day my new leadership trainer, a speech therapist, was working at the hospital and called in to see me. She must have told the others I was ill and lonely, and one or two others then popped in. Unfortunately, by this point I was becoming very low and seemed to have no energy to make them feel welcome.

The surgery went well physically, but emotionally I was suffering badly. The lady in the room next door was distressed at night, and her screams and crying haunted me and brought back distant memories from my past.

To my surprise, my sister came to see me. She had travelled all the way by train and I was amazed to see her, but also very disturbed. I wanted to make her welcome, but I simply burst into tears. She felt I was being ungrateful, saying over and over again, "How can you be miserable when I've come all that way?" I couldn't give her an answer or even organise a meal or cup of tea for her, and I felt very bad.

My shoulder was extremely painful and the surgeon couldn't understand how it was so badly damaged. He probed for answers but I blamed it on childhood injuries from sport and other activities. He said he'd had to rebuild the whole socket and fix the shoulder in place with criss-crossed muscle. I spent three months with my right arm strapped across my chest, which made balance hard so even moving around was tricky.

The post-operative period ended and I was ready for discharge. The nursing sister said I needed a lot of care initially because I mustn't fall and the arm had to stay firmly fixed to me. The big questions to address were where I should live and who would look after me. Jeannie needed to work, and so did most of my friends. The sister asked where my parents lived, and I told her about Dad's heart attack. She asked more questions, however, and established that he was now out of the woods. He, my Mum, and sister were home all day. The ward sister could see no reason why I couldn't go back to my family home. She talked with my parents and sister. It seems they couldn't argue with her so they agreed, but I was surprised and concerned that they felt they had been forced into this.

An older lady called Betty, who belonged to the Christian group and was a health visitor in the south, had originally come from the north. She was going home on my discharge date so she agreed to take me to my parents. She was very down-to-earth and had a healthy view of some of the group's practices, and she became a special friend and mentor. She was excited that I was a qualified health visitor and wondered why I hadn't gone straight into health visiting. She soon picked up on my lack of confidence. I said I'd gone into nursing because I felt I wasn't well enough trained to manage a ward, and she encouraged me to reconsider.

Betty and I chatted all the way home. She was a master of probing questions and was cross to find out that I'd been poorly cared for by the

Christian group while I was in hospital. She wanted them to take me into the training flat during my recuperation and promised to arrange it.

> *I'm aware that I'm writing "Betty this" and "Betty that". This expresses a sense of how distant I felt from all that went on. She organised everything for me, and was easy to talk to...*

I explained my family situation to her. She quickly grasped that I might meet some opposition when I got home so she gave me her phone number and told me I could call her if for any reason I needed to go back down south when she returned from her visit to her parents.

I hoped that wouldn't be the case but, sadly, it was. Although they'd said yes to the ward sister, my parents were furious with me. They said I was most unwelcome and refused to cook for me or help me in any way. They still needed to eat and so I didn't quite understand. I begged them to keep me until Betty went home again. I managed to help cook and wash up using my left hand. Mercifully, my balance was improving and I didn't fall. I was so sad to find myself so unwelcome. I felt homeless and vulnerable. I had no broom or chair to bar my bedroom door, but I couldn't have manoeuvred them anyway. Fortunately, however, Dad had to sleep downstairs and was low on energy so I was left alone.

I phoned Betty, who was cross with my family and upset for me. She contacted Georgia and they arranged for me to go straight into the training flat for a week. They said they'd make further plans after that.

I was sad when I left my family after such a tough few days. I had felt unwelcome before, but this time I couldn't do much to serve and please them so my being there just angered them intensely.

I got back to find that Jeannie was angry to have been left alone in the cottage. To add to my sense of rejection, I had also unknowingly upset a girl called Natalie, who had a room in the training flat. She was leaving to go and live at home and her leaving date was a few days away. She had a single room so it was decided I was to sleep in there. Betty had realised I'd overdone things at home, so she told my new flatmates I needed peace, rest, and at least a week in bed. When I arrived at my new lodgings, Natalie didn't want to speak to me because she'd been asked to go into a shared room for her remaining two days. The leader of the flat was kind but busy. She emphasised that I could only expect care for a week, saying, "This *is* a training flat." Betty was

163

angry with her and reminded her that she and Georgia, who were both more senior in leadership, would make the decisions.

None of this helped me in my fragile emotional state. My new housemates left me in bed all day and gave me a meal at night. I knew that I was a nuisance and took lots of painkillers which kept me asleep. Georgia and Betty knew that all was not well in my world. Mercifully for me, during my tough week in the flat, Georgia injured her ankle, and her kind response was to say, "Helen, you can be my legs and I can be your arms for the next six weeks." I was delighted to spend every day with her for six lovely weeks.

I still had to sleep in the training flat and soon moved into the shared room. Natalie left the house and Jeannie replaced her for a while. She and I shared a room, which was hard at first, but later we became soulmates.

My days with Georgia were such a blessing. She weaned me off the drugs I'd started to overuse to ease my emotional pain. Georgia had herself been rescued from a London drug gang and looked after, healed, and nurtured by two kind Christians after they led her to new life in Jesus.

One time after this the gang ambushed her, injected her with drugs again and tried to keep her with them. She told wonderful stories of how God had rescued her and kept her drug-free. She owed her life to Him and to Christian friends who led a community ministry in London. Georgia and Betty were pioneering something similar where we now lived. They were very mature and knew how the world functioned. They also knew the love of God in the depths of their being – each of them felt rescued by Him and wanted to spread that love to others.

The leader of my training flat was much younger and less mature. She had grown up at boarding school and learned to be hard and determined and to hide any negative feelings. Achievement was what mattered to her most. Georgia and Betty saw this and were helping her to learn a more tender approach. While she was still learning, however, life in the house proved challenging. My entry as an invalid left me feeling I needed to perform highly to prove myself. I was afraid I'd be thrown out of the house if I didn't play by the many rules.

33

I recover

Six weeks with Georgia left me seeking God and His love in everything I did and thought. She loved the psalms and saw Psalm 31 as her life story. I learned to read them until they touched my soul and spirit. I also learned to look at Jesus and how He loved and ministered, rather than simply following the harsh rules and methods laid down by the Christian group and some of its leading members.

I went back to my quiet Anglican church, where Georgia also worshipped. We couldn't go whilst she couldn't drive so I learned to spend longer times with God on the Sundays I had to stay at home. He always met me. I'd learned again to pour out my heart to Him and await His response. One of my favourite psalm verses was, "My heart says of you, 'Seek his face!' Your face, Lord, I will seek."[32] I was getting to know His smile.

After the six weeks of Georgia's recovery period were over, I was still on sick leave. I was feeling anxious about losing her, and God provided again when a Norwegian girl called Annya came to stay near Georgia for about six weeks. Georgia introduced us and we met and chatted and prayed together many times during those days. Annya was a lovely Christian with a healthy perspective to counter any rigid rules I might pick up. I was prone to look for rules and regulations, which I think came from my ritual training. I carried a deep need to get it right, which came partly from rejection, but that was to be discovered much later. At this point, God simply got me through – miraculously.

---

[32] Psalm 27:8 (NIV)

Dad recovered. Mum put huge pressure on me to spend long periods at home, but I withstood her manipulation. I could see they had survived while I was ill and so I chose when I went and how long for. I knew they would never be the nurturing, doting parents I'd longed for. I also knew I could not be responsible for them, although this was all head knowledge. God highlighted Psalm 81 to me one day, and used it to give me a sense of releasing Dad and the family to Him: "I relieved your shoulder of the burden; your hands were freed from the basket."[33]

All this helped, but through the summer Georgia had to work away a great deal. She was a national conference speaker now, and her household and my leadership trainer often accompanied her. I felt bereft and a very second-rate Christian in comparison. I was allowed to sleep at Georgia's while she was away with her household to look after her cat, Dobby. He was most unsociable and cross when his mistress was away, and woke me every morning at 6 a.m.

I was lonely, tired, and becoming disturbed by torment all over again. I decided to take a job on permanent night duty in the neonatal intensive care unit. This kept me away from people and free from jealousy and feeling undermined by my Christian friends. I loved working with neonates and often spent ten hours caring for one baby. Observations and treatment were every five or fifteen minutes. I was totally absorbed. The night staff were easy-going and were all qualified, so there was no competition.

Sleep was hard in the day so I bought myself various forms of medication. I needed to take more and more, but I didn't care so long as I slept. I took a shift which involved working eight days and then having six off, so I could go north for my days off. This seemed to please Mum, Dad, and Annabella. I also rode with my class of riding instructors on all my days off. Life seemed good.

I didn't give up on God but I did care less.

Mercifully, Betty, Georgia, and my house leader, Fran, picked up on my behaviour. Fran told me that if I wanted to stay in the training flat I needed to show greater commitment, and she was right. I was helping several young women in the community ministry, but my work prevented a lot of group involvement. Fran couldn't deny that the people I was overseeing were flourishing in their relationship with God. There was, I knew, a need for more of that.

---

[33] Psalm 81:6 (ESV)

Betty and Georgia challenged me to apply for a health visiting job. God confirmed this for me in several ways and I obeyed, even though I knew it would cause trouble at home. I also knew it meant giving up on horses, but God helped me there. I met a health visitor who loved riding and we started to ride together on a brilliant weekly ride for advanced riders. God never fails to care for us.

It's time to bring this book to a close. But before I do, it may amuse you to know that during my second depression I vowed to God that I would stay single. I thought this was because I had discovered His love so much more deeply during the dark days of the depression, and that I regretted my fall away from Him when I was on night duty and settled back into home and horses. It was actually because I was terrified of men, of intimacy, and of marriage.

I knew none of that until I met Steve. He also came from the north, and looked nothing like the dream husband I had imagined when Betty persuaded me to talk to God about my thoughts on marriage. He wasn't tall, or blonde, or blue-eyed, or sporty, but he was far, far more than that fantasy man. He expressed the love of God in ways that deeply touched my soul, and seemed to care for me and understand me. We met when we shared the same meeting room for his after-church student ministry and my nurses' ministry. We took our different leadership responsibilities seriously, but we always ended up chatting long after the meetings had ended and most people had left.

I agonised with God about my feelings for Steve. I ended up seeing the doctor again, who told me that I was lovesick and just needed to tell Steve about my feelings. God and my wise counsellors also said that God seemed to want us to develop our relationship – it seemed I would be more disobedient to God if I insisted on staying single.

So I told Steve and we eventually married. We've had four children together. We have had to climb mountains and weather valleys and deep, dark places, not least the death of our first baby, Joe, after only thirty minutes of life. Nearly four decades on, we are in ministry together and enjoying God more and more; we are proud parents, blessed in-laws and greatly privileged grandparents.

I can't begin to express how great God is – how loving, how kind, and how much He paid on the cross to live this life with us and redeem it in every wounded area, and for eternity.

Jesus, I love you so much. I'm forever grateful to you, my King, my Lord and my brilliant God.

Appendix

Spiritual strongholds: my testimony

I could never tell every detail of my story. I guess none of us could. We each have a story to tell. What follows is an article I was asked to write for a UCB book called *Overcoming*. It may offer a few more details and insights to those who are interested in my story, or have further questions they would like answered.

I wonder what comes to your mind when someone talks about "spiritual strongholds"? In some ministry I've seen shouting, screaming, coughing, and vomiting in the poor person receiving prayer. As for the ministers, I've seen them hassled and even injured.

I have myself been the subject of such prayer due to the level of demonic influence in my early childhood. These high intensity encounters and emotions really happen and illustrate the first key I discovered to breaking spiritual strongholds with respect and dignity intact both for those praying and those receiving prayer.

Spiritual warfare is a truth encounter not a power encounter.

Jesus won the victory over Satan when He died on the cross and took the keys of death and hell. Jesus conquered death by rising from the dead, and the enemy is under His feet. He has given us authority to cast out demons in His name and by the power of the Holy Spirit, but there are several keys to doing that with appropriate love and honour to all concerned.

Strongholds are built up in the mind, usually on top of wounding or trauma in a person's life. Culture and family history can also have an influence. Let me illustrate from my own life how a spiritual stronghold is built and dismantled.

My Grandpa taught me the truth about Jesus and His love for us by telling me stories of Jesus each season, and showing me the flowers that grow in those seasons. This was a beautifully simple way to teach a young child about God and His love for all He created and His way of salvation through Jesus.

Other villagers, including my grandmother and father, were enticed into demonic rituals through the fear of death. Many village children died of typhoid in the tainted water supply. A water diviner deceived them into believing all water would be safe if they did the evil things they were told to do. That's how I ended up abused and very ill-treated when I was out of Grandpa's watchful care. I wanted to follow Grandpa's Jesus but I was too afraid of Gran and the village to trust him all the way. My dad taught me in cruel ways that if I ever stepped outside his will and guidance, I and those I loved would suffer terribly.

This deceiving belief gained greater hold when a dear Christian farmer friend was killed by a car on the road in our village, when I was only three, in an accident in which his head was severed from his body. Grandpa was the village policeman, and he instructed my dad to keep me away from the scene while he rallied help. Instead, Dad, who was heavily involved in rituals, took me to look at my farmer friend and whispered, "This is what happens to people who follow your Grandpa's God." That trauma and threat lodged in my mind.

Many years later I had been rescued from the evil activity in the village, become a Christian and married a dear, godly Christian man. In our second year of marriage we had a baby whom we named Joe. He died after only thirty minutes of life. My trust in God was rocked by this but I tried to carry on my Christian walk, blocking out all my feelings and battling against the thoughts that said to me, "This is what happens to people who follow your Grandpa's God."

Having three lovely children in subsequent years helped me believe that God could be trusted. We led Alpha and Freedom in Christ courses. Things went well until one of our children became ill with a life-threatening condition.

Suddenly my trust in God plummeted and I even began to encourage my own children to be careful not to be too enthusiastic about Christianity.

I went away on retreat to try to seek God in my faith crisis. God led me to a vicar who knew how to deal with spiritual strongholds. He, my lovely husband, and I asked the Holy Spirit to help me see what had caused such a drop in faith for me, and we discovered that it was a spiritual stronghold built up from trauma upon trauma in my childhood, indoctrination with wrong beliefs about God, myself, and others, and a history and culture of fear in my ancestors.

By talking with me and letting me share all my arguments against God's truth, my wrong beliefs began to change. I started to see the fear and deception in what Gran and the villagers had taught and believed. The truth encounter was beginning to bring down the stronghold in my mind (2 Corinthians 10:4-5).

When we asked the Holy Spirit for the roots of this stronghold, the trauma of abuse, the experience of seeing my farmer friend in the road, and the loneliness and grief of losing Joe came clear. With my husband and vicar to love and support me I was able to express this pain. I experienced God's love and healing for them all, in a journey that lasted 18 months.

It wasn't easy. There were loud shouts and tears sometimes, but then Jesus also expressed loud shouts and tears in His lifetime (Hebrews 5:7). That wasn't demonic. That was pure emotion and the struggle to pioneer and perfect our faith by raising the courage to go through the way of the cross as His Father God led Him. He trusted that God would defeat the biggest enemy of death and God did that for Him – and for us.

He did it for me too. Where wounds and beliefs and our history keep us trapped, the enemy can invade and gain a hold. When truth, expression, forgiveness, and healing are allowed in, the enemy loses his grip. We begin to resist his lies. Then it's easy to come close to God and in Jesus' name and authority tell the enemy to leave us. He no longer has a hold on us. That's what I was able to do with dignity and respect from my vicar and husband.

Now that's what I love to do for others. In the words of James 4:7, "Draw near to God" (ESV) by embracing His truth. This truth encounter is resisting the devil and, as he cannot bear the light, the nearer we draw to God, the less the devil wants to follow and then he finally flees. Continue to come close to God and have Him reveal and heal the wounds that caused the wrong beliefs. I love how God comes close to His beloved children as is promised in that verse.

One of the most precious things God said to me in all my healing was: "I never wanted this to happen. Child, I love you. Child, I am always with you. Child, I will never leave you nor forsake you. No. Assuredly not."

No stronghold is too big for Jesus to bring down with love, respect, and dignity.

Similar Books by the Publisher

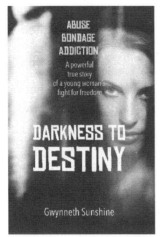

Darkness to Destiny
Gwynneth Sunshine
ISBN 978-1-911086-67-3

Gwynneth completed her education, not with great academic qualifications, but with a calling from heaven to reach out to the homeless and rejected with the love of Jesus. She invested herself in spending time with, and praying for, the marginalised, but her efforts soon led to burnout, followed by a rapid downward spiral emotionally and spiritually. She began to encounter Satanic activity, depression and sickness, along with abuse and rejection from those around her. At times she made poor choices. Gradually, she found herself drawn into the world of drug addiction, with poverty, suffering and violence. God seemed distant and Gwynneth found herself trapped beyond her ability to escape. But she could not forget her childhood encounter with Jesus…

Child of Mine
Marianne Edwins
ISBN 978-1-911086-57-4

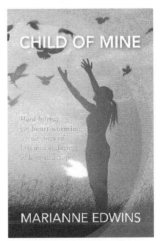

Marianne Edwins' early life was filled with broken relationships, unplanned pregnancies, severe financial hardships and faithless men, in an environment of crime, violence and misogyny. Increasingly her life lacked hope, lacked peace, lacked love. Then one day, on an ordinary walk in the countryside with a friend, she had a sudden unfathomable encounter that transformed her life forever. Soon Marianne would find herself setting up a ground-breaking charity to help the homeless, travelling across the world to show compassion to those in poverty and war-torn areas, and ultimately finding peace and closure in the most unexpected way.

Books available from all good bookshops and from the publisher:
www.onwardsandupwards.org